CW01646445

ALAN MANN'S

A–Z

OF

BUDDY HOLLY

To Charlie
Best wishes,
A 1994

ISBN 0 9524286 01

Copyright of the author, Alan Mann - 1994.

Publishers: The Sound of Tex-Mex.
Printers: Norwich Colourprint Ltd., Drayton, Norwich.

This book is dedicated
to the memory of
a good friend,
Trevor Manger.

First and foremost Buddy Holly's music needs to be listened to, with any dissection and analysis kept at a modest level. However, those that love Holly's music will always seek to translate that emotion into the written word. Hence this present volume.

Hopefully, it does not plagiarise the definitive 'Remembering' biography by Goldrosen/Beecher but is rather one fan's attempt to bring together most of the Holly-related material that has surfaced over the years and present it within a simple A to Z format.

It has been a labour of love that is willingly dedicated to all Buddy Holly fans throughout the world, both past, present and yet to come.

Acknowledgements

Sincere thanks to John Beecher for his help and encouragement in the year or so this book has been in gestation. However, the errors that have undoubtedly arisen are the responsibility of the author and reflect both his age and gathering infirmity.

Thanks to all my Holly friends and correspondents over the years who really are too numerous to mention — but they know who they are and will forgive not being listed individually. However Bob Dees (USA), Steve Derby, Lawrence Cross, Goff Pattinson and Peter Rodger (UK) must get an honourable mention and individual thanks for hanging in. Larry Matti has generously given permission to use the Green Bay photos if needed.

Love and thanks to wife Pamela and children Karen, Nicola and Richard who have tolerated their father throughout this project. (They surely understand that the word fan is an abbreviation of fanatic).

Lastly an extra thankyou to daughter Nicola who rashly volunteered to type the manuscript and did this superbly without neglecting her new baby Eleanor. Keeping it within the family, brother Graham Mann of Norwich Colourprint Limited has been a great help and is responsible for the cover design and for getting the words onto the printed page.

PREFACE

The problem in embarking on a work with the title of an A–Z of Buddy Holly is just what to include and — much more difficult — what to leave out. Individuals such as Bob Hale, M.C. at the final Surf concert, Don Webb, a recording artist who Buddy hoped to produce and even Des O'Connor are overlooked whilst perhaps more undeserving entries have crept in. Such are the pitfalls that lie in wait for any unsuspecting, budding author.

The fan of trivia may be disappointed that no lengthy discography is featured and there is a distinct lack of record Master numbers. Rather the book is an attempt to throw the net as wide as possible and come up with a readable, interesting volume that will supplement the excellent Goldrosen/Beecher biography of several years back. Hopefully, all genuine rock'n'roll fans should find something to interest them and even the most rabid Holly/Cricket follower **might** just learn something new.

I hope it finds favour. I have thoroughly enjoyed putting it together.

Alan Mann, Little Melton, Norfolk 1994.

INTRODUCTION

It's been a long time since 1957 and *That'll be the day*, although to some of us it seems like only yesterday - especially if you've had all the mirrors removed from your house in case you catch a glimpse of someone over fifty. But the fascination for rock'n'roll and all things 50's has remained strong even for those born long after that decade - in fact there are probably more rock'n'roll records and books available now than ever there were when the establishment was telling us that 'jungle music' would never last.

When Alan Mann told me he was putting together a book called *The A to Z of Buddy Holly* for his 'retirement thesis' I wasn't surprised for if ever there was to be a real labour of love, this would have to be it. Alan was a founder member of the Buddy Holly & Crickets fan clubs in the early 60's and his enthusiasm for the music and unearthing information about those artists has never diminished. This enthusiasm comes alive through the entries in this book and Holly fans can be certain of a 'good read' all the way from Abba to Zager & Evans. In between you're sure to discover all sorts of things you never knew, had almost forgotten, or didn't realise you ought to have known in the first place. In any event Alan's book is going to be a useful addition to the Holly and Crickets bookshelf and I for one am happy he's got it together.

John Beecher
July 1994

ABBA

This A-Z of Buddy Holly starts in unlikely fashion with an entry for Abba and ends with a short entry for Zager and Evans! But in between those two extremes there is much to interest any genuine fan of Buddy Holly so please read on.

Abba were the Swedish supergroup who met up in 1973 and carried all before them till they disbanded in the early '80s.

The connection with Holly is tenuous but group member Benny Andersson had, in an earlier incarnation, been a member of the top Swedish rock and roll group The Hep Stars, who recorded a ponderous English-speaking version of *"Tribute to Buddy Holly"* in the '60s.

"AIN'T GOT NO HOME"

Demo; recorded late '56, early '57 in Lubbock

This novelty track was the first US Top 20 hit for its composer, Clarence 'Frogman' Henry in January of '57 and it was almost certainly cut as a demo by Holly about the same time at the local Venture Studio in Lubbock. Buddy had just returned from his final Nashville session at Bradley's Barn in the November of '56 but continued to practice or record demos.

Holly's version first surfaced, heavily overdubbed on the 1969 'Giant' album but has been subsequently released in its raw state by Rollercoaster Records on their 1986 album 'Something Special from Buddy Holly'. Whilst neither version, in the normal way warranted a commercial release, they are of historical interest and a pointer to the type of material that influenced Buddy and the boys.

STEVE ALLEN

Bespectacled US TV host from the '50s who founded 'The Tonight Show' in 1954 and who was consistently critical of rock'n'roll. Nevertheless many classic artists of the genre (e.g. Presley, Burnette, Jerry Lee) guested on his popular TV series, 'The Steve Allen Show'. At one time Holly and the Crickets were rumoured to have performed on the programme but late night re-screening of the series has confirmed categorically that they did not appear.

Spookily, there is a 1956 Vogue Coral album by Steve Allen, the cover of which features his horn-rimmed glasses in a spotlight which is uncannily similar in concept to the original Holly 'Love Songs' album sleeve that was to appear 25 years later.

Steve Allen was much attracted to jazz, occasionally fronting his own big band or orchestra and it is unlikely that he and Holly ever met up. Allen had an instrumental hit in 1955 with his piano interpretation of *"Autumn Leaves"*.

JERRY ALLISON

Jerry Ivan Allison, known as J.I., was born on 31st August 1938 and co-founded The Crickets with Buddy Holly in early '57. Jerry is an excellent drummer who has worked with an assortment of artists throughout his long career; Eddie Cochran and The Everly Brothers being the most obvious examples. At one time was an intermittent West Coast session man - when not a Cricket - and an instance of this was his appearance on the 1972 Johnny Rivers album,' LA Reggae'. Has also recorded as a vocalist - see entry under IVAN.

Certainly Holly and Allison were real soul-mates and many of the entries in this A-Z apply as equally to Jerry as to Buddy. Fans wishing to keep in touch with J.I.'s on-going career need to subscribe to the quarterly Crickets File magazine. (The Crickets themselves put out irregular news letters from their US base).

Buddy Holly and Jerry Allison met around '52 when the latter was playing with a group called Cal Wayne and the Riverside Ranch Hands and they started playing together more and more. With Buddy playing rhythm-cum-lead guitar and Jerry's busy drumming patterns backing him, the two created a pretty full sound in the day's before amps resembled double-decker buses.

Jerry Allison is a talented and humorous individual, totally unlike the drummer portrayed backing Holly in the celluloid film of the '70s. To this day he retains the rights to The Crickets name.

As Jerry's name is synonymous with Buddy's cross-references could be numerous. But see especially IVAN and PEGGY SUE GARRON.

TOMMY ALLSUP

Born Tulsa, Oklahoma on 24th November 1931. Tommy was, for years the unknown 'Cricket' despite playing superb lead guitar on several of Holly/Crickets 1958 recordings. Tracks such as *"Heartbeat"*, *"It's So Easy"*, and *"Loves Made a Fool of You"* all feature Tommy. He had met Buddy Holly when both were at Norman Petty's studio in Clovis and was a natural choice to tour with Holly on those fateful '59 Winter Dance Party shows - the first tour Buddy had embarked on without having Jerry and Joe B alongside him since he had become fully established. Other backing musicians were Waylon Jennings on bass guitar and Carl Bunch on drums. Tommy is famous for giving up his seat on the fatal flight to Ritchie Valens following the flip of a coin. This episode was shown in a dramatic sequence during the Valens biopic , 'La Bamba'. Initially Allsup was also believed to have perished in the crash as his wallet was discovered amongst the debris.

Tommy Allsup has a fine western swing pedigree and this includes associations with 'Asleep at the Wheel' as well as producing an album by the legendary 'Bob Wills and the Texas Playboys'. Like Jerry Allison, has also fitted in an active career as a sought-after session man.

Now in his '60s he performed a solo spot on the 1994 tribute concert at the Surf Ballroom in Clear Lake. The first time he had returned there since that fateful time some 35 years before.

"ALMOST PARADISE"

This Norman Petty composition was a Top 40 record for both Lou Stein and Roger Williams back in 1957 while the actual version by the Norman Petty Trio failed to score.

UK Holly fans - to whom the title meant nothing - were bemused to see it listed in the UK tour programme as one of the tracks which was to form The Crickets repertoire. Who knows, perhaps it was an effort to secure performance fees by Norman?

Needless to say it was not featured on stage but The Crickets did perform several tracks that they never recorded - *"Great Balls of Fire"* and *"Be bop a lula"* being those most frequently cited.

"AMERICAN BANDSTAND"

TV series

Famous, long-running, US TV show hosted by Dick Clark that first put in a local appearance in 1952 but was not networked nationally until August 5th, '57. In an interview taken from the Crickets appearance on Tuesday, 28th October '58 (featured on MCA box set) Buddy gets quite tongue-tied talking to Dick Clark and explaining how he and The Crickets were going to travel home separately after their performance. The then unpublished fact that the Crickets were in the process of splitting up makes the awkward moment quite understandable - to us. The 'History of American Bandstand' book lists the tracks performed that day as *"Think it Over"*, *"Fools Paradise"* and *"Heartbeat"* whilst the audible evidence points to *"It's so Easy"*, with *"Heartbeat"* being performed the previous Saturday.

Even earlier the Crickets had made their US TV and Bandstand debut performing *"That'll be the Day"* on Monday, 26th August '57 - this date being just one week after the song had topped the US charts.

There is no film extant of The Crickets appearing on American Bandstand and the footage released on the 1986 Bandstand video is from the Arthur Murray TV programme in late '57.

"AMERICAN GRAFFITI"

Film

This was the title of a celebrated 1973 film that was set in small-town America on a late summer night in 1962. It featured a minimum of live music but had a superb soundtrack of mainly '50s rock'n'roll classics that translated into a brilliant soundtrack LP - briefly an album hit for MCA when released in early '74.

This was one of the first occasions - and to be condemned - where obvious Crickets recordings were released as 'Buddy Holly'. This began to happen more and more and reflected the fact that Holly's name was well on the way to achieving mythical status and therefore more identifiable to the record buyer. (It also separated Holly material from later Crickets recordings).

Incidentally, the film dialogue of 'American Graffiti' contained a memorable line - since enshrined in rock folklore - that rock'n'roll music had been going downhill ever since Buddy Holly died. Most rock scribes do, indeed, tend to regard 3rd February 1959 as a watershed. On this theme - see AMERICAN PIE entry.

"AMERICAN PIE"

Song title

Don McLean wrote and recorded this eponymous track in 1971 and it is true to say that it catapulted him from obscurity to chart success in dramatic fashion. It is a story in song which charts the path of rock music using as its starting point the drama of Holly's death on 3rd February 1959, whilst at no point did the lyrics overtly mention Buddy's name.

However, in numerous interviews at the time - and to this day - Don McLean pays tribute to the genius of Holly, and the 'American Pie' album which followed was dedicated to the late singer. Don McLean feels that he helped bring Holly's music back before the American public at a time when, in the '70s, his name was little remembered.

Although Don McLean is a folk-related artist he has frequently interpreted Holly material - excellent versions of *"Everyday"*, *"Maybe Baby"*, *"Fools Paradise"* and *"It Doesn't Matter Anymore"* are a random selection of his recorded works. Recently appeared at the annual Clear Lake tribute concert thus reinforcing the link with Holly.

CARROLL ANDERSON

Manager of the Surf Ballroom, Clear Lake, Iowa the final venue for three of the artists on the ill-fated Winter Dance Party tour. Anderson was the last person to see the artists and pilot Roger Peterson - alive after he drove them to the airport at nearby Mason City for the night flight to Fargo, close to the border of North Dakota and Minnesota. The time is usually quoted as 1.00 am on February 3rd.

Mr Anderson had the harrowing task of identifying the fatally injured occupants of the plane later the same day. Although the craft came down soon after take-off Carroll Anderson was not aware that a crash had occurred till he awoke later that same morning.

He stayed on as Manager of the Surf till 1967. For other information on the last flight see entries under BEECHCRAFT BONANZA, CIVIL AERONAUTICS BOARD and JERRY DWYER.

"AN EMPTY CUP"

Crickets recording - cut on the road, Oklahoma City; Sept '57

A Roy Orbison composition, in it's original state it came Buddy's way via Roy's association with Norman Petty at the latters Clovis, New Mexico studios.

Recorded by The Crickets whilst on tour with the mammoth 'Biggest Show of Stars for 1957' the boys had an enforced break in late September when the white acts on the bill were unable to appear in 'mixed' shows. Norman Petty - on tour with the Trio at that time - was able to meet with the 4 Crickets and set up his recording equipment in the Officers Club Lounge on the Tinker Airforce Base, in Oklahoma City and this number, together with three other tracks, were cut. The Picks voices were later overdubbed back in Clovis and the track duly appeared on The Crickets first US album, 'The Chirping Crickets'. This masterly release, with its superb front cover photo said to have been taken on the roof of the Brooklyn Paramount Theatre, is often included in all-time 100 album lists.

In the UK when Coral Records were desperately searching for something to release in 1964 following major Holly hits with *"Bo Diddley"* and *"Brown-Eyed Handsome Man"*, they put out two of the Tinker recordings (*"You've Got Love"* was the other) and the disc actually crept into the Top 40 singles chart.

Most Holly recordings have been covered time and time again - this one hardly ever. Certainly Holly's plaintive vocal could hardly be bettered.

THE ANGELIC GOSPEL SINGERS

(Margaret Allison, Lucille Shird, Josephine McDowell and Ella Mae Norris)

US gospel group from the Deep South whose recording of *"'I'll Be All Right"* was a Holly favourite - he had a copy in his record collection - and the song was played at his Lubbock funeral.

The number is heavily organ-based and it's melody had been referred to as similar to *"True Love Ways"*. But the similarity is tenuous and *"True Love Ways"* does not really plagiarise the original.

The Angelic Gospel Singers were popular for their down-home versions of old hymns and gospel tunes. These were sung to either organ or piano accompaniment and for a while in the early '50s, they were popular Gotham Records artists.

PAUL ANKA

Born Ottawa, Canada on 30th July 1941, Paul Anka came to prominence when he penned and recorded the US No.1 *"Diana"*. His musical career continues to this day. Perhaps most well-known for coming up with the lyrics to a French melody and calling them *"My Way"*- it remains one of the biggest selling songs of all time.

Wrote *"It Doesn't Matter Anymore"* and Holly included the tune in his last studio session at the Pythian Temple, New York on 21st October 1958. This session was the only one of Buddy's definitely to be recorded in a stereo format. (Although *"Early In The Morning"* was reportedly cut in experimental stereo).

Anka toured Australia in 1958 with the Crickets, Jerry Lee and Jodie Sands, on a bill which included Australian pop artist Johnny O'Keefe who had a local hit with the part-penned *"Wild One"*. Paul Anka and Buddy Holly formed quite a close musical friendship and it has even been said they would have paired up as a song-writing double act at some point. Who's to know?

The only sour note concerning Paul Anka is that he has from time to time been quoted as saying he was touring with Holly at the time of the fatal crash - this is patently untrue. Jerry Naylor has also made a spurious claim to have been a Cricket, with Buddy Holly! See separate entry, JERRY NAYLOR. See also *"IT DOESN'T MATTER ANYMORE"*.

APOLLO THEATRE, NEW YORK

Virtually every famous black act has played the Apollo, in Harlem, New York at some point in their careers. Famous way before the advent of rock'n'roll it nevertheless happily became a venue for rock package shows when they were the phenomenon of the moment in the mid-50s

The Crickets played there on the back of their first big hit (*"That'll be the Day"*) as part of a bill that comprised several major black acts of the day. The scene led years later to Jerry Allison and Tom Drake writing a screenplay, 'Not Fade Away', and the project nearly got off the ground in 1975. But the scenario of Holly and the Crickets playing the venue was used later to good dramatic effect in the screen biopic, 'The Buddy Holly Story'.

Although Buddy had strong country influences in Hank Williams and others it is arguable that the commercial black sounds of Ray Charles, Mickey and Sylvia, Bo Diddley and the rawer sounds of Muddy Waters and Little Walter were more influential to his burgeoning talent.

GEORGE ATWOOD

Neither George Atwood nor Don Guess are included in the thirty odd names of Crickets listed in John Firminger's excellent 1993 publication[1] but, if not, surely they are bubbling under, to use the pop-chart metaphor? Perhaps a revised issue might see them creep in as it has always been said that there are more Crickets than a dog has fleas.

George Atwood was for years a session musician in the Texas/New Mexico border area and backed several artists at Norman Petty's studio. In late '58 he played bass on the excellent *"Heartbeat"*, as well as on the *"Love's Made a Fool of You"* sessions.

Holly and George Atwood kept in touch and it is possible he would have been involved, in some way, with Holly in producing records. He still lives near Lubbock and is close to clocking up the biblical three score years and ten as this publication goes to press (1994).

AUSTRALIAN TOUR

The short tour of Australia in early '58 lasted but a few days although the musical impact of Buddy Holly and the Crickets on that smallest of continents was such that they spawned long term fan worship that exists to this day.

The performers - Paul Anka, Jerry Lee Lewis and his group, The Crickets, Jodie Sands and Johnny O'Keefe and his Dee Days - shuttled between four venues where they performed a total of ten concerts in only six days.

Australia was, in the late '50s, somewhat of a backwater in technological terms and a negligible amount of photo, film or interview material has surfaced since their visit. Rumours have come and gone that archive material exists but after all these years it really is extremely unlikely that any major find will occur.

A brief, poorly recorded interview with Australian DJ Pat Barton was released several years ago on the US album 'The Day the Music Died'.

---

[1] The Crickets - in alphabetical order.

AUTOMOBILES

It's really of minor interest what vehicles Buddy drove so skip this heading of you wish! I've heard of at least six different models of cars which seems incredible given we are talking about a short timespan.

However, Buddy started early, by borrowing - and denting - his parents autos. His first car was believed to be a '55 Oldsmobile, although stories that this was a graduation present seem wishful thinking. Other early vehicles, mentioned by brother Larry, are a '51 red Cadillac and a Chevrolet, exact model not known.

At the time of the Crickets tour which ended in October of '58 the group were using a yellow De Soto station-wagon whilst Holly was driving a new taupe (pink) 1958 Cadillac. At the very end of his life, only a few months later he was the owner of a pale blue Lincoln Continental.

Perhaps loosely under this heading we can mention the Aerial Cyclone motorbike that Buddy purchased in '58 when he had just come off a tour. The bike was eventually used by Buddy's father, Lawrence, before ending up being purchased by the Crickets and presented to Waylon Jennings. It is still on display in his personal Nashville museum.

As a postscript to the above whilst Buddy Holly never got to own a British vehicle Jerry, Joe B and Buddy paid a visit to the Austin Motors factory when over here on their '58 tour. This fact is hardly surprising as Buddy was a fan of 'speed' and had apparently also started flying lessons back home.

Note. The author would welcome any additional information under this particular entry heading.

FRANKIE AVALON

A Philadelphian born Francis Avallone in 1939, who sprang to fame at age seventeen with two Top 10 US hits during 1958. He toured with Holly that year in the 'Biggest Show of Stars - Autumn Edition and joined the '59 Winter Dance Party tour - along with Jimmy Clanton and Ronnie Smith - after the fatal crash took out three of the main headliners.

Buddy evidently once remarked to the singer: "Frank, I got to confess I bought only one of your records, "*De de Dinah*", and that's because it's dee-dee-darned good!". Now, Buddy once said he was a better comedian than Des O'Connor - I'll leave the reader to be the judge on the above flimsy evidence.

Avalon was never a big artist in the UK but he had a string of US hits and - strangely - his first US No.1, "*Venus*", entered the US charts exactly one week after the 'Winter Dance Party Tour' ended.

"BABY I DON'T CARE"

Recorded at Norman Petty Studios, Clovis, New Mexico, Dec '57

Jerry Leiber and Mike Stoller wrote this song for the 1957 Elvis movie 'Jailhouse Rock'. Jerry Allison mentioned recently that the track was one of Eddie Cochran's favourites and that was how the boys got to record it.

Its first release in the UK was as an album track on the 'Buddy Holly' LP Coral LVA 9085 where it was listed as *"You're So Square"*. It had reverted to the correct title for its 1961 single release and it became a sizeable hit - surprising considering the modest publicity that surrounded virtually all Holly's posthumous Coral releases over here.

We know that Buddy was heavily influenced by Elvis and this number is one of seven Presley recordings that Holly either tried commercially or covered as a demo. Buddy's version of *"Baby I Don't Care"* is terrific - play it now and marvel again at the fact that Jerry Allison's drumming is courtesy of a cardboard box! An example of Buddy and the group experimenting to get exactly the sound they required.

"BABY IT'S LOVE"

'Buddy and Bob' performance at radio station KDAV. Circa '54/'55

One of a clutch of demo recordings from the Buddy and Bob era that would certainly not have been released commercially were it not for the events of 3rd February 1959. As it was this track and nine others were released in the UK only on the 'Holly In The Hills' album in 1965 and such was Holly's popularity here that the album spent six weeks in the charts. (The odd track out on this collection was the plaintive, *"Wishing"*, a demo dating from much later).

It is difficult to establish from the dubbed mono release what has been obscured. Undubbed the originals with Sonny Curtis still audible on fiddle, probably sounded more country. Buddy's mother is listed as part composer on this track but it is rumoured that it was really penned by a J. Fautheree.

Incidentally, undubbed tapes of the 'Holly In The Hills' material does exist but it is doubtful whether a commercial release would be justified.

"BABY LET'S PLAY HOUSE"

'Buddy and Bob' recording, Nesman studio, Wichita Falls, Texas 7th June 1955

As with *"Baby It's Love"*, this track first surfaced on the 'Holly In The Hills' album but it is much more out and out rock'n'roll with Holly on solo vocals. Recorded in mid '55, Elvis had waxed his version on February 5th of that year, the original being by the blues singer, Arthur Gunter. When the Holly version first came out it was given the title *"I Wanna Play House With You"* and the country artist, Cy Coben was listed as composer. This was corrected on the later box-set release.

The Holly recording is quite dynamic and ought to be heard much more often. Deservedly made an appearance on the excellent Charly double album, 'Buddy Holly Rocks'. The overdubbing by Norman Petty is probably minimal on this and *"Down the Line"* which was recorded at the same Wichita Falls session.

"BABY WON'T YOU COME OUT TONIGHT"

Demo made at Norman Petty Studios, Clovis, New Mexico; Feb - Apr 1956

A self-penned tune that Buddy recorded as a demo several times during late 1955 and early 1956. The released version was recorded in 1956 at Clovis but did not surface in the UK until April 1963.

Cynical comment, no doubt, but Coral gleaned all the sales they could from the singles, *"Reminiscing"*, and *"Brown-eyed Handsome Man"* before finally releasing the album containing this and other new material. (Meanwhile impatient UK fans had imported the US album some two months earlier).

Sources indicate the track's alternative title is *"Moonlight Baby"* although such a phrase does not actually form part of the lyrics! In 1983 Steve Hoffman, then of MCA records, was instrumental in putting out an album of mainly early material which included this track in its pure unadulterated format.

In the event that a definitive box-set (CD or ANY format!) materialises then an unreleased version of this track would be a natural for inclusion.

DEAN BARLOW AND THE CRICKETS

Grover 'Dean' Barlow was lead voice of the Crickets. Confused? Well, any self-respecting Holly/Crickets fan knows that the 'other' Crickets were a R'n'B group from the early 1950's and had no connection with the later hit parade group.

According to their album sleeve 'The Crickets' on Jay Dee 5040, their producer Joe Davis earned a considerable cash settlement from the Texan group because of the latter's use of the title, The Crickets.

Anyone with wide musical tastes should seek out recordings by the Dean Barlow/ Crickets group. A million miles away from any definition of a Tex-mex sound they are, nevertheless, very listenable indeed.

BENNIE BARNES

Fairly obscure country performer. Whilst he cannot readily be traced in reference books he recorded one of the better tribute records with the touching title *"Gold records in the Snow."*

It didn't chart in the States and neither did a clutch of such records that marked the Buddy Holly plane crash. The exception was *"Three Stars"* by Tommy Dee, with Carol Kay and the Teen-aires, that climbed to No. 11 in early 1959 in the US, while Ruby Wright had the British hit. See also - TRIBUTE RECORDS.

THE BEATLES

The Beatles choice of name was influenced by that of The Crickets, while their early song writing style was partly inspired by the writings of Holly and his group. There is a lengthy entry under Holly's name in the weighty Ultimate Beatles Encyclopaedia - published by Virgin - which spells out several connections between the two groups.

The Beatles most commercial Holly recording was *"Words of Love"* which is a fairly faithful copy of the original. Earlier they had made a private recording of *"That'll be the Day"* the sole record of which remains in McCartney's hands. In their German period the Beatles had recorded 'live' versions of *"Reminiscing"* and *"Crying Waiting, Hoping"*.

Older Holly fans may recall reading in the musical press, circa 1968, that The Beatles had ordered a complete set of the MCA 'MUPS' albums of Holly's recordings. Earlier, in 1963, The Beatles had sent a congratulatory telegram to the post-Holly Crickets group who were enjoying a successful 'second' career and continuing to tour. (And they still are!).

Some of the better covers of Beatles material was released by The Crickets in the USA on a Liberty album entitled *"California Sun"*.

See also entry under - PAUL McCARTNEY.

"BECAUSE I LOVE YOU"

Demo made at Norman Petty Studios, Clovis New Mexico; Feb - Apr 1956

A plaintive ballad that was recorded as a demo in Clovis early 1956 and which saw its first release 7 years on as part of the 'Reminiscing' LP. The album had a long stay in the LP charts and the cover photo was worth the purchase price alone. (For any rare individual who does not have the original sleeve it is a silhouette of Buddy's head against the backdrop of an aeroplane window. A reversed copy of the photo was used on the later, 'Remember' album).

The released track was overdubbed under the guidance of Norman Petty and this created stereo masters which allows aficionados to sort out fairly clearly what instrumentation has been added. *"Because I love you"* was later released in undubbed form and more recently with backing vocals added by The Picks. The latter versions you either love or hate according to personal preference.

BEECHCRAFT BONANZA

The 10 year old light aeroplane, registration No. N-3794N that was totally demolished shortly after taking off from the Mason City airport, Iowa, on route to Fargo, North Dakota, 3rd February 1959 whilst transporting Holly, The Bopper and Ritchie Valens to the next stop on their Winter Tour.

For further details see entries under CIVIL AERONAUTICS BOARD report and JERRY DWYER.

JOHN BEECHER

This name is synonymous with that of Buddy Holly in UK circles, where he has always been in the vanguard of those fans who have promoted Holly's talent at every opportunity. He founded the first UK Buddy Holly Appreciation Society, which did so much pioneer work.

Now heads up Rollercoaster Records which is his main occupation within the music field. Has had numerous links with The Crickets over the years and even co-produced their '78 single *"Cruise In It"*.

Holly biographer and all round good-guy who is so modest he offered me money to delete this entry!

CHUCK BERRY

Born Charles Edward Berry, 18th October 1926 in Missouri, Chuck is one of the seminal figures in 1950's rock'n'roll who is still doing his thing to this day. Although in his sixties, he has bounced back from adversity more than once and his place in rock's Hall of Fame is guaranteed.

Mention is often made in passing that, when touring Holly and Berry used to shoot craps together. Certainly Joe Mauldin has been quoted as having very fond memories of Chuck Berry who was always ready to help in those far-off days. It all seems a far cry from the usual reclusive picture which is painted of Chuck.

Usually singer song-writers perform definitive versions of their own compositions but Holly's demo-style version of *"Brown-eyed Handsome Man"* rocks and flows, far better than Berry's original. Buddy Holly occasionally performed Chuck Berry material on stage but did not record anything of Chuck's apart from the demo mentioned above.

MIKE BERRY

Mike Berry is an ultra-talented singer, who from time to time has added acting to his repertoire. He has had two far-flung bursts of UK chart success, spanning twenty years; in the very early '60s and again in the early '80s.

Over the years Holly's vocal style has attracted many 'copy-cat' artists but none has got closer to the timbre or feel than Mike Berry. Added to that is Mike's known sincerity that has been there ever since he first auditioned *"Tribute To Buddy Holly"* for Holly fans prior to it's 1961 release. Has never actually recorded with the Crickets but has teamed up on stage from an early 'Sixties Crickets tour to occasional tribute events down the years. Was persuaded to belatedly visit the US and finally got to the Surf ballroom in 1992.

Mike's 1985 recording of Lee Jackson's *"Holly"* deserved chart success but sadly didn't get enough exposure. Earlier he had re-recorded *"Tribute To Buddy Holly"* for the outstanding 'Rocks In My Head' album which allowed him to brush up the lyrics and jettison that irritating opening line 'The snow was snowing . . .'.

A seriously under-rated artist who modestly remains dismissive of his own contribution to the Buddy Holly legend.

THE BIG BOPPER (J. P. RICHARDSON)

Lost his life in an Iowa cornfield alongside Buddy Holly, Ritchie Valens and the plane's pilot, Roger Peterson.

Jiles Perry Richardson Junior was born in Sabine Pass, Texas on October 24th 1930 and one can avoid later dates which are sometimes quoted. In this 29th. year at the time of the Winter Dance Party tour he was old in comparison with some rock'n'rollers whilst seeming youthful alongside Bill Haley and a virtual baby where Joe Turner was concerned. (Joe was 45 years old when he appeared in the film 'Shake Rattle and Roll' - a definite 'revived 45' if ever there was one.)

J.P. had started out as a DJ on local radio and was a programme director by the time he was released to tour - and cash in - on his monster hit *"Chantilly Lace"*. He had used his Big Bopper persona from a fairly early date and in his DJ work but initial discs came out with the description, Jape Richardson and the Japetts. *"Beggar to a King"* (1957) was one such release, but as early as 1954 Richardson had produced a Bopper-type demo *"Boogie Woogie"* which first surfaced in the UK on a Flyright album of material from Jay Miller's Louisiana studios.

The Big Bopper's Mercury releases were well recorded with first class fidelity. The music still jumps out of the speakers like a rock'n'roll version of Phil Harris. Of the twenty, or so, recordings left by the Bopper virtually all were self-compositions. He can also be heard to good effect on the answer record by Donna Dameron, *"Bopper 486609"* which was held back for release until October 1959. Exactly one year after his death his voice was on the UK hit parade courtesy of his backing grunts to his friend, Johnny Preston's big hit, *"Running Bear"*.

Deservedly books have since been written cataloguing The Big Bopper's career and short life for, in many ways, his story was every bit as tragic as that of Holly. Musically the world lost three stars in the early hours of 3rd February 1959.

"BLUE DAYS, BLACK NIGHTS"

First Nashville recording session at Bradley's Barn 26th Jan '56

The obscure 1956 UK Brunswick single 45 of *"Blue Days, Black Nights"* / *"Love Me"* is worth considerably more than the 6/- or so that fans remember paying for it light years ago. £100+ would now be little more than a bid that probably would not secure it, such is its rarity.

From the first Nashville session (January 1956) the track features a prominent, sharp-edged lead guitar performed by Sonny Curtis and with Holly's warm vocal it is, in the writer's opinion, one of his better and more underrated performances.

The song was written by singer-songwriter Ben Hall for Buddy with the idea that it would produce his first hit - instead it failed to make any impact outside of getting played on a few local juke-boxes. Ben Hall himself cut the original demo disc now available and released on a Rollercoaster C.D.

None of the three Nashville sessions led to any overdubbing so we hear the track the way it was put down. The exception is a 1984 version with backing voices added by The Picks - see separate entry under their name for general comments on those performances.

"BLUE MONDAY"

Practice Tape; recorded in Lubbock late '56/early '57

This number was a major US hit for Fats Domino in January of '57 having been performed by him in the film 'The Girl Can't Help It', just a few months earlier. Holly's performance dates from early '57 and is very much a home-type version, although it was recorded at the local Venture Studio in Lubbock. As with *"Ain't Got No Home"* it was first released in 1969, as part of the 'Giant' album, heavily overdubbed. Comparing that stereo release with the later undubbed mono release (Rollercoaster Records) reveals just how comprehensive is that dubbed instrumentation. Although in most instances the undubbed recordings are superior, in the case of *"Blue Monday"* the drumming is overpowering and this distracts from Holly's vocals.

Buddy was a big fan of his fellow-artist, Fats Domino and whilst it is frustrating that he did not make a fully commercial recording of *"Blue Monday"*, he did fortunately, record another Domino/Bartholomew composition *"Valley of Tears"* as part of his first solo album. It was a deserved double-sided hit in 1961 spending fourteen weeks in the charts.

"Blue Monday" by Fats was so distinctive that covers seemed non-existent at the time. It is surprising to note that ten cover versions of it are listed in the 1990 book 'Who Sang What in Rock'n'Roll'. Amongst the ten was a Crickets version for their 1962 album 'Something Old . . .' that is quite listenable but still pales in comparison with the original.

"BLUE SUEDE SHOES"

Practice tape; recorded late '56/ early '57 in Lubbock

It is an amazing fact that Carl Perkin's *"Blue Suede Shoes"* was his one and only US top 40 record, yet, several decades later, he remains one of the great legends of rock'n'roll.

Buddy Holly made a practice demo of it, probably in early '57, and it eventually saw the light of day - with other new material - on the posthumous release of the 'Showcase' album. All of the tracks were heavily overdubbed and an official release of the unadulterated tapes had to wait a further twenty-two years (LP 'Something Special'/Rollercoaster).

Buddy's version is frantic and it was a tune he frequently used on the bandstand in live performances. The released track - in either format - does not do Holly justice and is for completists and die-hard rock'n'rollers only. As if to back up these subjective comments the track itself rarely appears on Holly compilation albums.

BO DIDDLEY

Artist

Born Ellas Bates in 1928 and later adopted the name McDaniel, Bo is one of the key figures in the birth of rock'n'roll and he's still doing his thing today even if a trifle self-indulgently. In his career had one minor Top 20 hit only and has never been able to cash in fully on rock unlike some of his contemporaries.

His name has become synonymous with the 'Bo Diddley beat' and numerous artist have used it to good effect including Holly and Allison who wrote *"Not Fade Away"* with part composer credits going - not to Bo Diddley - but to Norman Petty. (Whilst Petty's contribution on a number such as *"True Love Ways"* seems quite believable composer credits on such as *"Not Fade Away"* seems bizarre).

In a reverse compliment Bo Diddley recorded a very creditable version of *"Not Fade Away"* on a London Sessions album in 1976. Not many connections between these two great artists but Bo Diddley had a hand in composing *"Love is Strange"* which Buddy taped in January of 1959 just days before embarking on the final tour - see song title entry LOVE IS STRANGE.

See next entry - *"BO DIDDLEY"* - song

"BO DIDDLEY"

Hit version recorded as demo/practice tape, Norman Petty Studios, Clovis, New Mexico approx. Dec '56

1963 was the year that Holly's posthumous career was re-activated and *"Bo Diddley"* was a Top 5 entry in June having been released as a follow up to his earlier hit, *"Brown-Eyed Handsome Man"*.

No need to list composer credits on this track and Buddy's hit version was recorded at Clovis in 1957 although with heavy overdubbing later by The Fireballs, a hit instrumental group in their own right. The undubbed version - sounding a bit sparse without the lead guitar riff - came out on the Steve Hoffman inspired MCA album 'For The First Time Anywhere' in 1983.

Another, much looser, version of *"Bo Diddley"* was recorded by Buddy as a demo a month or two earlier and makes for interesting listening. Buddy calls out 'break time' to drummer Jerry Allison mid-way through what is very much a rehearsal-type track. Die-hard fans should endeavour to seek out this hard to find original version. See also entry -BO DIDDLEY; artist.

PAT BOONE

Born Charles Eugene Patrick Boone in 1934, the singer is a direct descendant of frontiersman Daniel Boone and had numerous US hits in the early days of his career (1955 to 1962). He seldom gets a good press when mentioned in rock literature mainly because his earliest recordings were felt to be sanitised versions of the earthier originals by such as Little Richard and Fats Domino.

A cutting remark of Holly's allegedly made in '57 was that Pat should be in the background on records making the 'doo-wop' sounds! That humorous but rather flippant remark was surely not meant to be taken literally - Pat Boone was a stylish vocalist who added his own small contribution to the panoply of rock'n'roll. (But having listened again to Boone's version of Domino's *"The Fat Man"* perhaps Holly had a point!).

There is little else to connect the two artists, although they were contemporaries. Pat Boone recorded a decent version of *"That'll be the Day"* on his 'Great! Great! Great!' album in the Sixties. The two singers were really coming at rock'n'roll from opposite directions and of course, Pat Boone rarely got involved on the composing front.

DAVID BOX

This has to be one of the saddest entries in this book as David Box lost his life in circumstances uncannily similar to his inspiration, Buddy Holly, while flying near Nashville, in 1964.

Born in Sulphur Springs, Texas on 11th August 1943, he actually got to record with the Crickets at just seventeen, when he did lead vocals on the back to back tracks *"Peggy Sue Got Married"* and *"Don'tcha Know"* which was the group's last Coral single and disappointingly, was not a hit. I remember the great difficulty had in purchasing the disc, as well-intentioned record shop stop staff insisted the recording was by Buddy Holly! (His version was still out and had been a modest hit in late 1959.)

David went onto make a few singles before setting out on his own fateful 'plane journey. His life has been well researched by well known Holly-scribe John Ingman - David Box deserves to be remembered and certain of his recordings do crop up on occasion. (As I write an excellent compilation containing several David Box tracks remains in catalogue on Rollercoaster - 'Hep Cats from Big Spring').

OWEN BRADLEY

The legendary Nashville producer who's association with artists reads like a 'Who's who' of country music. Born in 1915, it really started back in 1947 and although now retired as staff producer with MCA, he produced independently up to recent times. Having originally produced Patsy Cline, he had the weird sensation in 1981 of producing her two *"duets"* with the late country great Jim Reeves.

Was Holly's first real producer when he had overall responsibility for three sessions that Buddy cut for US Decca in January, July and November of '56 at Bradley's studio in Nashville. Certainly the sessions were not a commercial success but the acrimony portrayed in the celluloid movie was pure Hollywood. The music itself was not at all bad and deserves a special, if small niche in the history of rock'n'roll.

It is often forgotten that Owen Bradley had a major hit with his quartet in 1958 with *"White Silver Sands"*. If he hated rock'n'roll he hid it well when he cut an excellent set of instrumentals such as *"Raunchy"*, *"Big Guitar"* and others.

A musician, producer and Nashville executive - Owen Bradley is a highly talented individual.

"BROWN-EYED HANDSOME MAN"

Hit version recorded as demo/practice tape. Norman Petty Studios, Clovis, New Mexico, Dec '56

As with the *"Bo Diddley"* track Buddy cut two versions of this Chuck Berry number within months of one another. The earlier, weaker version was a demo recorded in Lubbock late '56 and it was not released until the 1980's, on a Roller-coaster album. The hit (overdubbed) version was recorded in Clovis early '57 and the main lead guitar line is Holly's own. It is arguable that the undubbed '57 version (on 'For the First Time Anywhere' LP) could have been a hit, as originally performed. That most certainly would not have been the case with the *"Bo Diddley"* track which - undubbed - lacked the strong guitar hook.

"Brown-eyed Handsome Man" was the second biggest solo hit for Holly reaching No. 3 in 1963 and no doubt helped the 'Reminiscing' album - which featured the single - have a very successful chart life.

A copy version is seldom better than the original (and as a demo Holly's was not a 'copy' as such), but there is little doubt that Holly's hit version is better than Chuck Berry's original which was the 'B' side of *"Too Much Monkey Business"* and not one of Chuck's strongest recordings.

'Handsome Man is a good example of the music Buddy and the boys performed live in the early days and it's good to have the performance captured for all time on disc.

DAVE BRUBECK

Born in California 1920 Brubeck was an innovative, white US jazz pianist whose career stretches back to the 1950s and who is still on the scene some forty years later. Fronted the Dave Brubeck Quartet and had a run of hits in the UK in the 1960s the most famous of which was *"Take 5"*. Pictures of Brubeck from that date show him wearing heavy framed glasses.

Allegedly had a little-reported friendship with Holly who he said was very knowledgeable on the modern jazz scene(!). Brubeck visited Buddy back-stage at the Palladium in March 1958 when he stopped off from an extensive world tour and it must have been quite a horn-rimmed occasion.

Brubeck was reportedly shattered by Holly's death and in a 1962 interview bemoaned the fact that they never got to record together. All this seems rather unlikely, however and the links between Holly and Brubeck have not been corroborated and seem somewhat embroidered.

BUDDY AND BOB

This was an early formation (circa 1953) that comprised Buddy Holley - as spelt at that time - Bob Montgomery and Larry Welborn. The latter was later to become a member of the Four Teens - see separate entry. Buddy, Bob and Larry performed at functions and on Radio KDAV prior to Buddy getting his big chance to record in Nashville. On one notable occasion in 1955 they got onto a local bill headed by Bill Haley which helped Buddy's embryonic career no end.

The group's calling card at that time used the descriptive phrase 'Western and Bop' which is a pretty good summary of the facts. Most of the music they 'recorded' in 1954/1955 is taken from local radio broadcasts or rehearsals. An album full of Buddy and Bob material came out as 'Holly in the Hills' in 1965. On reflection it's a great pity the album was not released as performed by Buddy and Bob. The LP is quite homogeneous except for the mysterious inclusion of *"Wishing"* - although it was probably added because composer credits include Montgomery's name. (But see comments under *"Wishing"* on this point).

The group were a legal entity for a time with Hi-pockets Duncan as manager but they ceased to exist once Buddy went to Nashville.

See also BOB MONTGOMERY entry.

BUDDY AND JACK

In 1952 (even before Buddy and Bob) Buddy teamed up briefly as a duo with a Lubbock youngster, Jack Neal, and they performed without great success on a local TV talent show. Much in the style of the Everlys we are told.

Later Jack was replaced by Bob Montgomery and the group became 'Buddy and Bob'. Jack Neal eventually left the music business but retained connections and surprisingly made his first commercial recording as late as 1980.

He is not known to be playing on any released Buddy Holly material but he did record two demos which he states feature Buddy on guitar.

THE BUDDY HOLLY STORY

Album

This memorial album was available for years after its 1959 release and by 1970 had sold one million copies resulting in Buddy's parents receiving a gold disc. The original LP is still well placed on the list of all-time UK chart albums.

The sleeve notes for both US and UK albums were penned by Ren Grevatt of the Music Business magazine. Four years later he was to write similar respectful sleeve notes for a Patsy Cline album that followed her death in yet another light plane crash.

Keep an eye out for the alternate UK album cover. In the early 1960s a different black and white photo - fuller faced - was used on the front cover for a short period and this print has become quite collectable.

This quite classic album contained all the hits to that time (except for *"Listen to Me"*) while, in addition, two classic *"B"* sides, *"Everyday"* and *"Raining in my Heart"* were deservedly included.

THE BUDDY HOLLY STORY

Film

An Innovisions - Eca production which was made in 1977 and had its premiere the following year in Dallas, Texas.

A book of the same name by John Tobler came out in the UK shortly thereafter and contains a lengthy illustrated section on the film. The book was presumably an attempt to cash in on the film but sales were modest. A soundtrack album died the death too probably helped by an ITV strike that precluded advertising at the critical time. Another factor could have been that superb twenty Golden Greats of Holly/Crickets material had rocketed to No.1 on the album charts for three consecutive weeks and - thankfully- creamed off the main sales.

It could be argued that the film biography was a genuine attempt to bring Holly to the big screen. But the bulk of Holly aficionados feel it was long on poetic licence and short on fact. One thing not often in dispute is that Gary Busey gives a sincere and hypnotic performance in the title role and was deservedly nominated for an Oscar. But at 33 years of age he was (for some) unconvincing in playing the life of an 18-22 year old. It must have also been a calculated decision not to use one of the greatest rock voice's, Holly's own, on the soundtrack.

On a sad note Robert Gittler - who wrote the screenplay - committed suicide just before the premiere of the film's release. For those who can't stomach the film - play *"The Real Buddy Holly Story"* by Sonny Curtis - it's all there in just over three minutes of musical magic.

"BUDDY'S GUITAR"

Taped at Holly's New York flat Jan '59

This is the untitled instrumental listed in the appendices of the 'Remembering Buddy' biography. It is just over one minute in duration and is based on the Ray Charles number *"Leave My Woman Alone"*. Holly would have been familiar with it from that source although his friends, the Everly Brothers, had also recorded a fast-paced version.

Holly's tremulous electric guitar strumming was recorded on his Ampex tape recorder during January of 1959. The snippet has never been released commercially but will perhaps one day take it's place on a definitive Holly box set. It is however possible to obtain it on a European bootleg LP 'The Apartment Tapes'.

"BUDDY"

The Musical

World-wide hit musical that is now in it's fifth fantastic year in the West End having been written by Alan Janes as an antidote to the inaccurate film biography. The musical still manipulates the story a touch but all is forgiven in what can only be described as a glorious celebration of Holly's musical legend that is designed to appeal to the popular masses. This it surely does.

At one time or another Joe B, Jerry Allison, Vi Petty and Maria Elena, have all been and seen the musical. But whether they enjoyed it any more than the film is somewhat debatable.

The show needs to be seen and enjoyed for what it is - a nostalgic knockout that helps to keep Holly's name alive in these ebbing years of the 20th. Century.

CARL BUNCH

Carl was the drummer with Buddy on the last tour but by the time the artists reached the Surf Ballroom, Clear Lake he was already sidelined in hospital with frost-bite brought on by travelling in a rickety tour bus through the frozen Northern states of the US.

Tommy Allsup - who agreed to play lead guitar - had been asked by Buddy to contact a drummer he had met at Clovis one time. This was Carl Bunch who was with Ronnie Smith and the Playboys at the time. Bunch has never ever failed to acknowledge that he and Waylon were not 'true' Crickets but just backing up Buddy who had plans to link up again with Jerry and Joe.

Carl Bunch today is involved in church work and has been quoted as saying that he sincerely believes Buddy Holly's death was brought about by the Devil as Buddy would have eventually led a musical crusade to bring people back to Christ(!). An amazing comment that may raise eyebrows but which cannot be dismissed.

"God works in mysterious ways his wonders to perform".

JOHNNY BURNETTE (AND THE ROCK'N'ROLL TRIO)

A legendary rockabilly artist - and no mean composer - who sprang up in the late 1950's and eventually became a successful pop balladeer before his premature death. This was the result of a fishing accident and it is ironic that this took place at Clear Lake . The Clear Lake in question - one of many in the US - is in California and about 1500 miles due west of the Iowa version.

Although both from the South and both Coral artists at around the same time (1957) it is unlikely that the paths of Burnette and Holly ever crossed. At the time when Holly was doing most of his touring Johnny was in Hollywood trying his hand at song writing.

Johnny Burnette was born 25th March 1934 in Memphis and died 14th August 1964. Much too early in the scheme of things. Sadly his brother, Dorsey, bass player with the trio in the early years, also died prematurely in 1979 (age 47) the result of a heart attack.

The family name carries on with children Billy and Rocky Burnette both in the music business.

GARY BUSEY

Actor Gary Busey played the lead role in the major film biography of Holly in the late Seventies, having a few years earlier started rehearsing the part of J I Allison for the abortive film 'Not Fade Away' - please see brief entry under the film title.

Busey (arguably too old at 33 to play Buddy) had a musical background and fronted a group called Carp for several years. Later, calling himself Teddy Jack Eddy, he backed singer Leonard Cohen. Busey played his own lead guitar in the Holly film and the soundtrack numbers were put down 'live' in an attempt to capture the spirit and energy of Holly.

Busey had a serious motorbike accident a few years ago and, ironically it was announced on the BBC that the accident was fatal. This reader - one of many - was under the misapprehension for several months that the part of the late Buddy Holly had in fact been played by the late Gary Busey! Happily Busey survived the shunt and, after being hospitalised for months, eventually resumed his acting career.

Whether or not one likes the film biography it has to be said that Busey gave the role his all and tried hard to research the part to get inside the character of Holly. It has been said that the result (musically) was more like Gary Busey plays Chuck Berry.

See also entry under film title THE BUDDY HOLLY STORY

GLEN CAMPBELL

Born 22nd April 1936, Arkansas, USA

A contemporary of Holly's but their paths didn't actually cross.

Campbell was to become one of Capitol's major recording artists with hits spanning twelve years (1967-1978 inc.). His inclusion in this volume is through his connection with the Crickets. He played on several of the group's Liberty recordings in the early '60s.

Glen Campbell had the unusual distinction of briefly backing Gene Vincent (although not a real Blue Cap) as well as having a stint with The Champs following the departure of Dave Burgess. Had a prolific career as a session man before his solo career took off.

RAY CAMPI

Legendary rockabilly artist virtually unknown in his home country (USA).

From the South, he manufactured an introduction to Norman Petty at Clovis in 1958. Spent time looking at the set up Norman had, the hope being that Petty might decide to manage him.

Ray knew of Holly and contacted him around that time with songs that he had written - the possibility being that Holly might be tempted, however nothing materialised at that juncture but possibly something might have done further down the line.

After the accident Ray Campi helped compose two tribute songs - one specifically about the Bopper - and these were commercially released but were not hits.

TINKER CARLEN

A friend of Holly's from Junior High school days - they were pals and as embryonic musicians also jammed together. This was in the days when Buddy was also running around with Bob Montgomery, Don Guess, Larry Welborn and others.

Tinker was never a formal group member but (from his telling) just kind of hung out. Probably cruising around Lubbock looking for the Hi-D-Ho drive-in? In fact, he teamed up a few years ago with Buddy's brother Larry and actually wrote a song entitled just that: *"Looking For The Hi-D-Ho"*. (The Hi-D-Ho was established in 1948 and it's still in existence and Sherry Holley - Buddy's niece, has performed there).

The epitome of a good old Texas boy Tinker Carlen has been around at many of the Lubbock events that have been connected with Holly over the years. Still hanging out.

RAY CHARLES

Ray Charles was born Ray Charles Robinson in Georgia, USA on 23rd September 1930. An all-time great of the music business who has travelled a long road since he first made records which were little more than attempts to impersonate Nat Cole.

Holly was a big Ray Charles fan and it is a matter of record that he wanted to link up with Charles and record a gospel-type album at some point. Of course it 'takes two to tango' and whether it would have come to pass is a matter of conjecture. But Charles has always been progressive and willing to experiment. So - who knows? Buddy and Maria Elena did try, unsuccessfully, to call at Ray Charles' home in late '58.

Whilst Buddy Holly and Ray Charles never happened as a duo did you realise that ironically, there is a tenuous link between the names? It seems that some of the posthumous apartment tape tracks of Buddy's were overdubbed by The Ray Charles Singers - the white hit vocal group of that era and not to be confused with Charles own group, The Raeletts.

One other snippet - of the 'did you know?' category. Although the track *"What'd I Say"* was not a US hit until July '59 Ray Charles had been performing it in his act for some time and it has been written elsewhere that Buddy did get to hear this classic song a few months before he died. An uncorroborated story which one hopes is true. See also JESSIE STONE entry.

CIVIL AERONAUTICS BOARD REPORT

An investigation into the fatal Iowa crash under the auspices of the CAB started within hours of the wreckage being discovered.

The basic facts are that the light plane, a Beechcraft Bonanza N-3794 N, owned by the Dwyer Flying Service was involved in an accident in the early hours of 3rd February 1959 approximately 5 miles Northwest of the Mason City municipal airport, Iowa. The accident resulted in fatal injuries to pilot Roger Peterson and his three passengers, well known entertainers who were headlining a Winter Dance Party troupe.

The purpose of the flight was to take the singers to Fargo in North Dakota upon completion of their show at the Surf Ballroom in Clear Lake on the evening of February 2nd. The actual flight take off was estimated at 00.55 am, February 3rd with the crash time being put at one o'clock or shortly thereafter. The demolished craft was found at 09.35 am on the farm of one Albert Juhl - the ground having a covering of light snow and the weather conditions being poor.

The body of the pilot was in the wreckage whilst the bodies of Holly, Valens and the Bopper were close by. All had, without any doubt, died instantly.

The final report of the CAB in September '59 attributed the main cause of the accident to pilot error.

See also entries under BEECHCRAFT BONANZA and JERRY DWYER.

JIMMY CLANTON

Born 2nd September 1940 Clanton was a teen-idol type (a la Fabian, Avalon etc.) who surprisingly emanated from near the Crescent City of New Orleans. Was drafted, with others, to replace the dead artists on the fateful Winter Dance Party tour of '59. His 1958 release of "*Just a Dream*" was to be his biggest.

Co-incidentally he met Ritchie Valens when both appeared in 'Go, Johnny, Go' the rather tepid 1958 rock'n'roll movie. Publicity stills from that time show a surprisingly chunky Ritchie Valens chatting near a Dansette-style record player to Clanton. The latter looked the archetypal pop star whilst Valens looked - well, different.

Jimmy Clanton is currently (1994) performing again after a lengthy absence from the music business. He has been a church minister in the course of his life.

DICK CLARK

Dick Clark remains the world's oldest teenager having been born on 30th November 1929. Host of the US TV show American Bandstand, that started in '52 and which clocked up well over 30 years before it ran its course.

Dick Clark comes over as slick and professional but wisely never nailed his colours solely to the mast of rock'n'roll. This stance - and Clark's longevity in the music business - stands in stark contrast to the life and career of his contemporary, Alan Freed.

Buddy Holly and the Crickets appeared on American Bandstand in '57 and again in '58. See entry under heading, AMERICAN BANDSTAND and for contrast see entry under ALAN FREED.

JUNE CLARK

From Lubbock, Texas and was sister of Donnie Lanier, lead guitarist with Buddy Knox - see separate entry.

Although not credited on the record label June Clark helped out with the backing vocals on the hit recording of *"That'll Be The Day"/"I'm Looking For Someone To Love"*.

Buddy Holly, backstage at Green Bay, Wisconsin, 1st Feb. 1959.

CLOVIS, NEW MEXICO

Clovis - I learnt recently - is the name of an ancient French saint and who knows perhaps he gave his name to this small New Mexico town where Norman Petty worked his magic.

The original studio where Holly and The Crickets cut the bulk of their recordings still stands but is mainly used these days as an 'historical' venue where occasional visitors tour and perhaps ponder on the sounds that once vibrated within the walls.

Petty had a newer studio built nearby many years later and this is a more high-tech operation where recordings are still made although both the Petty's are sadly no longer alive (see separate entry under their names).

EDDIE COCHRAN

Born 3rd October 1938 in Minnesota, USA this classic rocker died 17th April 1960 while on tour in the UK. Although he appeared on bills in the States with Holly and they were reported as close friends, no photos of the two together have ever surfaced. The Eddie Cochran Historical Organisation failed to trawl one in their brief existence. Anyone out there got one? (There is a photo of Eddie with members of the Crickets but Buddy is not pictured. Jerry Allison's own collection of personal photographs from the early days were unfortunately lost many years ago).

Buddy was known to feature Cochran numbers in his stage act and certainly both *"Summertime Blues"* and *"20 Flight Rock"* were performed on the Australia tour. It has been said that The Crickets were short-listed to appear in 'The Girl Can't Help It' film but the idea was ruled out by Norman Petty. A pity, if true.

One of the saddest recordings ever has to be Eddie's version of *"Three Stars"* - his tribute to the three dead rock stars and royalties on which would have been diverted to relatives of the deceased artists. His emotional version did not get released at the time but surfaced in the '60s as an album track.

Session guitarist, superb vocalist, multi-instrumentalist Eddie could do almost anything musically and his early death at 21 was a rock'n'roll tragedy of the first order.

ED COHEN

Must be included as the man who brought Holly's life to the big screen. The film ('The Buddy Holly Story') has its critics but it has certainly helped Holly's posthumous career greatly. That big plus, must cancel out all the little minus points that the film racks up by virtue of the major inaccuracies that litter the script.

"COME BACK BABY"

Session at Norman Petty Studios, Clovis, New Mexico inc. King Curtis on sax 10th Sept '58.

One of those little known Holly recordings that really deserves to be more widely heard. Composed by Fred Neil, a New York songwriter, with Norman's name added, it was one of the two solo tracks that Buddy recorded in late '58 on the Clovis session where he enlisted the help of sax great, King Curtis.

The track didn't appear on disc until 1964 when it was one of several 'new' tracks on the 'Showcase' album. Whilst sources indicate the recording is overdubbed the fact that the track is in mono leads to the conclusion that additions are, in fact, minimal. (An undubbed bootleg version has surfaced on a European album of Holly material in the last few years).

Its a real pity that *"Come Back Baby"* is hardly ever included on compilations of Holly material as the vocal is first rate even if the composition itself is less than memorable. (Whilst ruminating - wouldn't the four Holly/Jennings/Curtis tracks sit nicely on a 7" vinyl extended play disc?)

SAM COOKE

Late, great, soul singer who we tend to think of as a '60s artist, his greatest days dating from 1960 when he joined RCA. In fact he was some two years older than Holly and had a string of big US chart records throughout the late '50s on the Keen label.

Originally a gospel singer he fronted the Soul Stirrers before his career took a different direction. It is surprising that Cooke is portrayed in a cameo role in the film biog. of Holly and also (by inference) in the 'Buddy' musical as, in reality, the careers of these two famous artists never apparently interconnected.

Sam was born on 22nd January 1931 in Clarksdale, Mississippi and died in Los Angeles after a shooting incident, 11th December 1964. Rumours about the strange manner of his death have echoed down through the years.

One minor link between Holly and Cooke is that both were backed briefly at one time by the great saxophonist King Curtis.

THE CORBIN BROTHERS

Larry, Sky and Ray 'Slim' Corbin were three brothers whose names are intertwined with that of Buddy Holly.

The brothers acquired the K-triple Lubbock radio station in the late '50s and it was there that Slim Corbin and Waylon Jennings helped Holly compose - on the spot - a number entitled *"You're the One"*. The hand claps which feature prominently on the undubbed version of the song are those of Corbin and Jennings.

Slim Corbin is deceased but brother Larry was instrumental in getting Lubbock to honour its famous son in the '80s when an impressive bronze sculpture of the singer was unveiled.

See entry - RADIO KDAV AND KLLL

'COUNTRYWISE' LP

Famous and scarce, 10" Dutch album which came out in the '60s and comprised of eight of the so-called Buddy and Bob numbers. Most of these are country in style except *"I Wanna Play House With You"* and *"Down The Line"* which are closer to rock'n'roll.

The album is highly collectable but most fans will have to settle for the counterfeit version which is easily identified. (Of the many differences between the two the original sleeve is glossy while the later, counterfeit one is distinctly dull in texture).

The superb front cover photo is taken from Holly's last New York photographic session at the time when Buddy's wife Maria Elena was becoming actively involved in helping to run his career.

EDDIE CRANDALL

A Nashville talent scout, long deceased, who was persuaded to watch Holly perform (as the Buddy and Bob trio) on a 1955 concert bill in Lubbock, which involved Marty Robbins - an act that Crandall himself managed at that time.

As a direct result Crandall requested that Holly send four original recordings to him in Nashville with a view to getting a record contract sorted out. This led to the somewhat abortive 1956 Nashville recordings for Decca. An important step in the story.

MARSHALL CRENSHAW

Latter day US artist who had a lowly 1982 hit but is little known in the UK although some material has been released here.

In 1987 - looking more like Elvis Costello - he played the part of Buddy Holly in the 'La Bamba', Valens bio-pic. Performed only one number in the film (and on the soundtrack) and the choice of material was strange. *"Crying, Waiting, Hoping"*. This was one of the New York apartment tape numbers that Holly was working on prior to the final tour but which he certainly did not perform live on stage.

THE CRICKETS

Lets keep this entry reasonably brief and remember that this book is about 'Buddy Holly and the Crickets' and the group's career post-1959 is not touched upon in any detail. To follow the continuing career of the post-Holly Crickets you can do no better than subscribe to The Crickets File which still appears regularly under the energetic guidance of John Firminger, a lifelong fan and friend of the group.

Back to the beginning. In 1957 some of us purchased a shellac 78 rpm disc of *"That'll Be The Day"* which contained the simple form of words, The Crickets with Orchestral Accompaniment. What a deceptive description that was! Early fans had little idea just who The Crickets were and if there was an orchestra involved maybe our ears were playing tricks on us. Eventually, we learnt that the group comprised of four surprisingly young men, Buddy Holly, Jerry Allison, Joe B Mauldin and Niki Sullivan. (In two errors on the first album sleeve Mauldin was listed as Maudlin and Lubbock ended up as Bullock).

By the time Buddy and the boys were performing in the UK Niki Sullivan had left and was striving for solo stardom with little success. (He went under the name of The Hollyhawks at one stage so made no attempt to hide his influences).

More than half of this book's content COULD be listed under a Crickets heading but hasn't been, so as to avoid duplication. I would refer readers to individual entries under group members names, but remember, there are more Crickets than a dog's got fleas.

"CRYING, WAITING, HOPING"

Taped at Holly's New York Flat, 11th Dec '58

Holly composition that he recorded at home on the Ampex tape machine he had purchased from his original mentor, Norman Petty. The simple tape features Holly and his acoustic guitar accompaniment and this original version still awaits a legal, commercial release. (It is however easily obtainable via a European album entitled 'The Famous Apartment Tapes').

Holly's vocal was overdubbed by Coral producer, Jack Hansen, within six months of the artists death and as the flip of *"Peggy Sue Got Married"* it was a sizeable UK hit in late 1959. Several years later Norman Petty overdubbed the track with heavy instrumentation and without any backing vocals. Both dubbed versions are on the '79 Box set on MCA records.

Unfortunately, stereo masters of this and *"Peggy Sue Got Married"* do not exist.

KING CURTIS

Born 7th February 1934, Died 13th August 1971

King Curtis was christened Curtis Ousley and he and Buddy were fellow Texans who were both operating out of New York in late '58. Curtis, was an incredibly talented saxophonist who backed literally hundreds of recording artists over a career that spanned many years but which was cruelly brought to an end when he was murdered in Harlem during August of 1971 (That year was a sad one for '50s fans as we also lost Clyde McPhatter, Dickie Valentine and Gene Vincent - all of them premature departures).

John Goldrosen wrote most descriptively in his original Holly biography of how Curtis, Waylon Jennings and Buddy all came together in September '58 for a recording session that was unique but, in a way, abortive. Norman Petty and Buddy were about to split and this led to Petty physically holding the masters from the session despite Holly owning the recordings.

The gem of the session was Holly's version of "*Reminiscing*" which resembles a duet between him and King Curtis. At the time of its release the composer credits were listed as 'King Curtis' but it has since been revealed that it was a Holly composition passed to Curtis as part of the deal for the session.

The legend of King Curtis is such that up to 20 years after his death a regular newsletter about him was produced entitled, appropriately, The Boss.

King Curtis was tragically stabbed to death trying to help break up a street fight in New York. A practice not to be recommended.

SONNY CURTIS

Where to start such an entry? Basics are that he was born in Texas, 9th May 1937 and is alive and well at this writing. Sonny's career has for most devotees never fully escaped the Holly connection and I don't think Sonny himself would argue that point to any great extent.

The link started very early - circa 1954 - when Sonny played violin on early Holly demos and carried on to the Decca days when he appeared on two of the three studio sessions playing either rhythm or lead guitar.

To the uninitiated that might appear to be it - in fact Sonny was a regular member of the post-Holly Crickets both as vocalist and as guitarist. Sonny still visits the UK on a pretty regular basis as a solo performer and time and again he demonstrates what an incredibly talented individual he is. Thus far we have not mentioned his song writing ability which is quite phenomenal. He wrote the classic Buddy Holly number *"Rock Around With Ollie Vee"* and among a wealth of material for The Crickets themselves such numbers as *"More Than I Can Say"* and *"Baby My Heart"*. He wrote the evergreen *"Walk Right Back"* for the Everly Brothers in 1961 and as late as 1989 co-wrote the No.1 US country single *"I'm No Stranger To The Rain"*. It is a great shame that Buddy Holly never got to perform The Sonny Curtis Songbook. Something taken from us in February '59.

On a personal level Sonny Curtis remains an unassuming and laid back individual and is one of the nicest people connected with the legend of Buddy Holly. If you haven't time to read Buddy Holly's biography and don't want the distortions of the film biography then listen to Sonny sing *"The Real Buddy Holly Story"*. It's all there - wrapped up in a 250 word song lyric.

BOBBY DARIN

Born Walden Robert Cassotto on 14th May 1936, in the Bronx, New York, Bobby Darin became quite a legend himself and it was a tragedy that he was not strong physically. He eventually succumbed while undergoing heart surgery back in December 1973. His own mother had died in '59 and his father before Bobby was born.

The paths of Holly and Darin crossed rather briefly in 1958 which led, fortuitously, to Buddy covering the Darin compositions *"Early in he Morning"*/*"Now We're One"*. Darin's version of the 'A' side was a hit (under artists name, Rinky-dinks) and both Holly's and Darin's versions entered the US charts the same week of '58.

Interestingly, each recording fell off the charts during September just a few weeks before both artists joined the same tour, The Biggest Show of Stars for 1958 - Fall edition. That fact is rather intriguing and one wonders whether there was any rivalry between the two singers. The fact that royalties from both versions went to composer Darin makes it unlikely however.

At Buddy's Texas wedding in August, '58 his own version of the Darin composition, *"Now We're One"*, was played. Whilst Buddy never got to collaborate with Ray Charles, Darin- on the same label at the time - got to record a whole album of Ray Charles material.

Before Bobby's death on 23rd December 1973 he had also completed at least 15 major film roles.

SKEETER DAVIS

Country artist who originally performed as part of a female duo, The Davis Sisters whose promising career ended in 1953 when Betty Jack Davis (no relation) was sadly killed in a road accident that badly injured Skeeter (shades of Vincent/ Cochran).

Skeeter Davis was born Mary Penick in 1931 and after the accident opted for a solo career having a major hit in 1963 with the haunting *"The End Of The World"*. In 1967 she recorded a tribute album 'Skeeter Davis sings Buddy Holly' on the RCA label. The session was produced by Felton Jarvis and Waylon Jennings (an RCA stable-mate) was used to play guitar on the recordings. Buddy's parents, Lawrence and Ella Holley attended the recording session and penned touching sleeve notes for the album.

Critics felt that Skeeter's light voice didn't suit the material and the album wasn't a success. Nevertheless it came out in the '60s at a time when Holly's name was little remembered in the US and this project, along with others, did help to ensure that his music wasn't totally forgotten.

We know Holly is fondly remembered by fellow artists and - in addition to Skeeter - albums dedicated to him have been recorded by Bobby Vee, Denny Laine, Matlock, The Hollies, Don McLean, Jimmy Gilmer and Tommy Allsup to list a random few.

"DEAREST"

Taped at Holly's New York flat, Jan '59

Composer credits on this apartment tape track are listed as Ellas McDaniels (aka Bo Diddley) Prentice Polk and Mickey Baker of Mickey and Sylvia fame. Strangely, the Holly version first saw the light of day dubbed John Barry - style as the flip to *"What To Do"* which was re-issued in 1963 on a UK Coral single. Initially the record label stated that composer credits were 'unknown' and as a result, the composition was given the unusual song title *"Ummm, Oh Yeah"* - this approximating to a phrase in the lyrics.

The undubbed version features just the Holly vocal and his acoustic guitar accompaniment and was included in the MCA box set. (There is another take - featuring slightly heavier strumming - and this has only come out on the bootleg-style 'The Apartment Tapes' album).

A second overdubbed version with a far fuller backing and intrusive vocal group appeared on the long-awaited 1969 album, 'Giant'.

Holly's plaintive vocal is one of his very best and the song deserves to be more widely heard than it has been - although it was included in the excellent 'Love Songs' album several years back.

JIM DENNY

At one time General Manager of the Grand Old Opry he was also a music publisher (Cedarwood Publishing Co Inc.) and booking agent who was involved with Eddie Crandall - see separate entry - and others, in helping Buddy get his first recording contract with Decca, in December 1955.

Jim Denny's Cedarwood held the original copyright on the sheet music for *"Modern Don Juan"* and *"Ting-a-Ling"*, etc. although it is doubtful that it earned them anything much in royalties.

Denny died over twenty years ago and unlike contemporaries such as Owen Bradley, was unfortunately never interviewed in any depth on his part in the Holly legend.

JOHN DENVER AND OTHER FOLKIES

The Rocky Mountain wonderboy was born 1943 Henry John Deutschendorf, junior, in New Mexico and his connection with Holly is tenuous as their careers didn't really overlap.

However, John Denver studied in Lubbock at Texas Tech in '61 and eventually got around to recording a Holly composition (*"Everyday"*) for RCA in 1972.

Have never stumbled across a quote by Denver pertaining to Holly which is somewhat disappointing given that Buddy's vocal style must surely have been an influence -even if only subconsciously.

Other artists who fall into the same category are Neil Diamond and Jim Croce. The latter singer, ironically, was killed in a small plane crash while completing a concert tour - Croce also composed the evocative *"New York's Not My Home"*; New York being Buddy's transplanted home at the time of his own death. Croce's music was occasionally used as the backing link in the US TV 'Reminiscing' documentary on Holly's life.

Completing the host of folk artists who have sung Holly's music are Joan Baez, Tom Rush, Phil Ochs and Carolyn Hester, not forgetting Don McLean who is the subject of a separate entry, under *"AMERICAN PIE"*. There may well be several others that deserve mention under the folk heading.

MURRAY DEUTCH

Small but important bit part player in the Buddy Holly legend and his name is usually coupled with that of Bob Theile - see separate entry.

Murray Deutch was with music publishers Peers-Southern and was instrumental in helping get *"That'll Be The Day"* launched on the road to success.

Mentioning Peer the publishers, above, leads me to mention that Elizabeth and Ralph Peer the 2nd, put out probably the earliest US Holly biography in 1972 when their book, 'Buddy Holly a biography in words, photographs and music' was published.

THE DIAMONDS

Canadian vocal quartet that shot to fame in early '56 when they made the US Top Twenty with a cover of the Frankie Lymon and The Teenager hit *"Why Do Fools Fall In Love"*.

Thereafter they consistently covered recordings by black vocal groups finally achieving a million seller with their version of *"Little Darlin'"* which completely eclipsed the original by the Gladiolas.

Mercury surprisingly issued the Holly composition *"Words Of Love"* as their follow up and this reached lucky thirteen in the Billboard charts. Buddy's version on Coral issued at the same time failed to even enter the top 100.

Both The Diamonds and The Crickets appeared on the same Alan Freed package show in the Spring of '58. Thereafter The Diamonds jumped on the dance craze and took *"The Stroll"* to No. 4 in the June before disbanding in the early '60s following several changes in personnel.

BO DIDDLEY

See under BO DIDDLEY.

DION

Dion di Mucci, born 18th July 1939, was backed by the Belmonts and were on the fateful last tour with Holly and the others. We tend to forget that up to that point they had not had a major hit so were more a supporting act singing doo-wop. It was in the '60s that Dion's career really took off and he garnered a string of Top 10 hits, mostly as a solo act.

The singer was quoted in contemporary interviews as being completely choked at the tragic loss of his good buddy, Buddy.

Dion di Mucci is still about - sporting a baggy cap as headgear - and is usually back to support - act status these days. Toured the UK in the '90s on a bill headlined by Dave Edmunds who had produced Dion's 1989 comeback album.

FATS DOMINO

Legendary New Orleans artist, born 1929 who is still rocking away almost 40 years after he first entered the US Top 10 (1955) with *"Ain't That A Shame"*. A track that high-school student Pat Boone covered and wanted to release with the more grammatically correct title *"Isn't that a Shame"*! He was eventually persuaded to use the original phraseology to everyone's great relief.

Buddy grew up a big fan of Fats and it must have been a tremendous thrill to end up on the same Paramount bill in New York as a fellow headliner. Holly did a demo of the Domino composition *"Blue Monday"* in '56 and this first surfaced on the 'Giant' album. The only Fats number that Buddy recorded commercially was the excellent album track *"Valley of Tears"* in 1957. This must have pleased manager Norman Petty as the number is heavily organ based and he performs the solo accompaniment. The track was recorded for the original Coral LP 'Buddy Holly' LVA 9085 at brother Larry's particular request.

Incidentally, I still have my copy of that album with a biro price mark indicating the cost as £1-15-9 1/2d. (Younger readers should consult their local reference library for a translation).

Held in high esteem by his contemporaries both Elvis and Ricky Nelson also recorded Domino material in the '50s.

"DON'T COME BACK KNOCKIN"

First Nashville recording session at Bradley's Barn, 26th Jan '56

Buddy collaborated with local Lubbock song-writer, Sue Parrish, to write this track and *"Love Me"* both of which were recorded at his first Decca session in early '56. UK fans got to hear the bulk of those Nashville tracks courtesy of two Brunswick extended play records that were presumably released directly as a result of Holly's sad demise in early '59.

In late '55 Holly had twice cut demo versions of *"Don't Come Back Knockin"* at the Nesman Studios in Wichita Falls, Texas. A version cut on 7th December 1955 was one of the acetates - see EDDIE CRANDALL entry - and these were released by Buddy's brother, Larry, on an extended play disc on his own Holly House label several years ago. As with the Bo Diddley track this earlier version is looser and has Holly calling out 'Let's play it again boys, let's go'.

The Nashville recording has also been released with added backing vocals by The Picks.

"DOOR TO MY HEART"

Buddy and Bob performance at Nesman Studio, Wichita Falls, circa '54/'55

Early demo recording of a Bob Montgomery composition that was released in 1965 as part of the 'Holly in the Hills' album. All the recordings feature some overdubbing but as the release - and all subsequent ones - have been of mono masters just what is added is not certain.

With Sonny Curtis on fiddle this track, and others, are mostly country-orientated recordings.

"DOWN THE LINE"

Demo recording made at the Nesman Studio, Wichita Falls Texas by Buddy and Bob, recorded mid '55

This track is a great slab of rock'n'roll and the nearest Buddy and Bob get to a duet. The composers were Holly and Montgomery themselves and visitors travelling across country in Texas/New Mexico will have no difficulty in understanding the inspiration behind the track's title phrase - to get anywhere you need to travel down the line.

As with other 'Holly in the Hills' tracks there is an undefined amount of instrumental overdubbing on the released recording.

Another quieter-paced version of *"Down The Line"* by Buddy and Bob has been released but on an album not sanctioned by MCA records.

"DROWN IN MY OWN TEARS"

Part only, taped at Holly's New York flat, Jan '59

This Ray Charles number was recorded by Buddy on his tape recorder in January of 1959 but subsequently the bulk of the track was taped over and the final few emotive lyrics only have survived. This fragment was included on the unsanctioned 'Apartment Tapes' album that came out on the appropriately named Prism label a few years back - if you don't know why see entry: PRISM RECORDS.

A version of the same song was recorded in Fort Lauderdale , February 25th 1958 with Buddy's vocals being backed by Jerry Lee Lewis on piano. This recording - of quite reasonable quality I understand - does exist and it is a pity that it has not been made available to Buddy's long term fans. Perhaps, one day, it will. (A Lewis-Holly duet of the Ray Charles composition, *"Hallelujah I Love Her So"*, is also believed to exist).

'HIPOCKETS' DUNCAN

William Joseph Duncan was a radio announcer from around Lubbock who was very helpful to Buddy Holly in the very early days. In a seemingly informal way he was manager to Buddy, Bob and Larry Welborn when they were a trio (Buddy and Bob) and trying to get spots on local shows.

Hipockets left his job on Radio KSEL in 1953 to set up what was probably the first all-country station Radio KDAV, from Lubbock, Texas. In his later days he ran KRAN radio station in Morton. Texas which he sold in 1979.

There is a convoluted explanation for his nickname but I prefer to assume its the more obvious reason!

Sadly Hipockets died on 21st December 1981.

JERRY DWYER

Hubert J Dwyer was the owner of Dwyer's Flying Service from which the doomed Beechcraft Bonanza was chartered by the artists for their abortive flight from Mason City to Fargo, North Dakota.

Understandably Jerry Dwyer has been reluctant to be interviewed in the years since the crash which was fully investigated by the US Civil Aeronautics Board and to whom he gave a four page deposition the day following the accident.

Putting it in perspective, whilst the musical world lost three stars in 1959 Jerry Dwyer lost a good friend and colleague in pilot Roger Peterson - see entries under the pilot's name and also under CIVIL AERONAUTICS BOARD report.

"EARLY IN THE MORNING"

Recorded at The Pythian Temple Coral Records Studios, New York 19th Jun '58. Backed by Coral session musicians.

Woody Harris - who had written *"Queen Of The Hop"* and *"Pity Miss Kitty"* - collaborated with Bobby Darin on this number which, for legal reasons, was originally released by Darin under the pseudonym, the Rinky-dinks. Holly's version came out at the same time and both were US chart entries in late 1958. It was to be Buddy Holly's last hit there during his lifetime.

The vocal has to be one of Holly's most powerful ever and it is complemented by the driving tenor sax sound of Sam 'The Man' Taylor and the black gospel group, The Helen Way singers adding backing vocals. So whilst we never got to hear Holly cut a gospel-style album we do get a flavour with this particular number.

Recording sessions in those days often comprised a minimum of four tracks being cut. On this occasion just two tracks were recorded (*"Early in the Morning"* and *"Now We're One"*) specifically with a single release in mind. Evidently recorded in stereo it is sad that a mono master only exists.

As Holly's recording did not reach the top 10 here or Stateside it is not always included in Greatest Hits compilations. A pity, as this has to be one of his greatest ever recordings.

DUANE EDDY

Born New York, USA, 28th April 1938

Famous 'twangy' guitarist who had a whole slew of hits in both the USA and the UK starting in 1958 with the distinctive *"Rebel Rouser"*. Most of the legendary recordings of Duane Eddy are those with the small Jamie label before he signed with the giant RCA label.

Possible - but no means certain - is that Holly and Eddy met up but, regardless, they still have several links which a few illustrations will suffice here.

In his time Eddy has produced recordings for both Phil Everly (one of Holly's closest friends) as well as Waylon Jennings when backed by the latterday Crickets. The Jennings/Crickets grouping were responsible for a particularly fine medley of Holly numbers which was put out in the '70s on one of Jennings albums which was also released as an RCA single.

Duane Eddy was voted Top Instrumentalist several times in UK polls and incredibly, Holly himself featured in such polls. This had to be a direct result of Holly's guitar playing which had been seen up and down the country in March '58.

DON AND PHIL EVERLY

Don born 1st February 1937: Phil born 19th January 1939

It is well-known that The Crickets and The Everly Brothers were firm friends. Although the singers all came from the South they actually first met on tour in Canada in 1957. Not only did they do one or two tours together but on one occasion the Crickets formed the back-up band for the Everlys.

Fortunately (unlike the case with Eddie Cochran) there are several photographs of Buddy with Don and Phil from those early days. The bond seemed particularly strong between Buddy and 'baby boy Phil', and the two got together in late '58 to jointly produce a session for little known singer Lou Giordano - for details see entry under singer's name.

Around the same period, Holly and his life-time friend Bob Montgomery composed *"Love's Made A Fool of You"* and *"Wishing"* in the hope that the Everly Brothers would record the numbers. Sadly this did not happen but Holly himself cut superb demos of both numbers that were finally released in the '60s.

Both Don and Phil took Holly's death badly and Phil was one of six pall bearers at his friend's Lubbock funeral on February 7th. But the link has survived Holly's death and Jerry, Joe B and Sonny backed the Everly Brothers in their 1960 tour of the UK. Into the '90s we find ex-Cricket Albert Lee playing lead guitar on Everly Brothers live concerts indicating the longevity of the links between the two groups.

"EVERYDAY"

Recorded at Norman Petty Studios, Clovis, New Mexico 29th May '57. Trio are supplemented by Vi Petty - Celeste.

This recording is an absolute gem and according to Jerry Allison was recorded quite quickly, at the same session as *"Not Fade Away"* was cut. Jerry's contribution? -slapped knees! Anybody who has tried to pick this melody out on a keyboard will know how simple it is - but how effective. Composed by Holly and Norman Petty the use of a celeste gives it a distinctive sound and it has become one of the numbers most associated with Holly throughout the years. Although it was never a chart hit (it was the 'B' side of *"Peggy Sue"*) it has nevertheless always been included in all of his Greatest Hits - type compilations. (It was eventually a UK hit courtesy of Don McLean in 1973).

In 1984 The Picks did overdubs to Holly's vocal but for many fans the uncluttered charm of the original was destroyed.

Buddy Holly cut a promotional radio jingle for Lubbock radio station KLLL to the tune of *"Everyday"* and all 28 seconds of it appeared on a controversial Live Gold album entitled 'The Real Buddy Holly Story' in 1991 - see separate entry, JINGLES.

TERRY FARLAN

An absolute unknown who cut an album of Holly's songs and this was released on the UK budget Hallmark label in 1969.

The heavy framed glasses the singer is sporting look as if they are being worn purely for the album cover photo. Terry Farlan was in good company as artists such as Brian Poole, Cliff Richard and John Lennon all had periods in their early careers when they sported Holly-type specs.

Terry Farlan could still be about - I know not. He seemed to surface just long enough to cut this album, which as covers go, was a reasonable effort.

IRVING FELD

Feld was president of Super Enterprises and with two others formed the General Artists Corporation (GAC) in the '50s, GAC were responsible in the US for staging many of the legendary rock'n'roll package shows that often featured over a dozen acts - each performing only 2/3 numbers.

In the UK, with far fewer stars, we had to tolerate a mixed roster of artists who often appeared on bills that bore more than a passing resemblance to their music-hall predecessors. The UK Tour that Holly undertook was an extreme example of the phenomenon. The bill - complete with the de rigeur compere - was 100% variety acts - one could be forgiven for thinking that the Crickets were added as an after-thought.

Irving Feld remains a shadowy figure and was certainly at the business - end of things. There have been rumbles down the years that the fateful tour should have been cancelled after the crash took out the headliners. Instead it carried on, with a patched up itinerary, through to the final February 15th date. Feld has long since retired but his son is in the music business carrying on the family name.

THE FIREBALLS

A quartet led by George Tomsco, lead guitar, who first hit in late '59 when their instrumental *"Torquay"* was a Top 40 hit. They had been formed some two years earlier taking their name from the fact that their staple live number, played again and again was *"Great Balls of Fire"*.

The group recorded at Norman Petty's Clovis, New Mexico studios and it is well documented that they came to be involved in a whole batch of posthumous overdubs of Buddy Holly material. Sometimes these overdubs have been criticised as turning Buddy Holly material into *"singalong with the Fireballs"*. But its very much a matter of personal opinion as to whether this was the case or not. What is certain is that the opportunity to include Jerry Allison or Joe B in on such sessions was missed. A matter of perennial disappointment, surely.

The Fireballs did meet up with Buddy Holly fleetingly when both were visiting Petty's Clovis, New Mexico studios in 1958 but their musical liaison did not crop up until after Holly's death.

The Fireballs added a vocalist, Jimmy Gilmer, in 1961 and this is the subject of a separate entry under his name.

FLATT & SCRUGGS

Lester Flatt (born 28th June 1914) and Earl Scruggs (born 6th January 1924) were definitive bluegrass performers who were members of the Grand Old Opry during the '50s and they were one of many influences on the youthful Buddy Holly growing up in Lubbock, Texas.

It is worth mentioning that for every white, country influence on Buddy (Hank Williams/Bill Monroe, etc.) there was seemingly a compensatory black rhythm influence in the shape of Fats Domino, Little Richard, Muddy Waters etc.

Holly seemed to distil all these varied inputs and come up with his own unique sound that has permeated down the years and seems as valid today as when it was created.

Flatt and Scruggs continued to perform as a duo until 1969. Lester Flatt - the older by 10 years - died in 1979 but Earl Scruggs continued to record as The Earl Scruggs Revue, although he has latterly moved away from active performing.

"FLOWER OF MY HEART"

Buddy and Bob performance at Nesman Studio, Wichita Falls, Texas. Circa '54/'55

One of a batch of five country - or western and bop - numbers that Buddy and the boys performed in the early days and they were probably recorded as demos at the Nesman Studio in Wichita Falls, Texas. Although not strong commercial numbers they were, fortunately, preserved for posterity. There is some overdubbing on each of the numbers and this was added for their release on the 'Holly In The Hills' album.

"Flower Of My Heart" was written by friends Bob Montgomery and Don Guess and although the number won a school prize, being chosen 'Westerner Song of the Year', it is not noticeably stronger than any of the other material.

Quite who wrote what on these earliest Holly/Montgomery tracks is very uncertain to say the least. Mostly authors had to be allocated when the recordings were given a commercial release, except in those few cases where a song had already been published.

"FOOL'S PARADISE"

Crickets recording following Niki Sullivan's departure. Cut at Norman Petty's Clovis New Mexico, Studios,. Probably 14th Feb '58

Norman Petty added his name to this composition by Sonny LeGlaire and Horace Linsley and The Roses were used to dub backing vocals for the finished release. This was the first time that Petty had switched from The Picks when looking to dub Crickets material. With the addition of distinctive piano played by Vi Petty the recording is a good one and it was surprising that it did not appear in album format until the 1971 release of *"Remember"*, which tidied up several loose ends at that particular point in time. (Notably being the inclusion of the Norman Petty overdubs of apartment-tape material).

The released master of Paradise is take 3 and undubbed takes 1 and 2 have circulated for a year or so on a bootleg-style LP on the Laroc label. Quite a coincidence that this spells Coral backwards!

Not a song that has inspired frequent covers but Don McLean did do a strong version on his 'Playin' Favourites' album in 1971. *"Fool's Paradise"* has been used as the title of several other songs - of most interest to rock'n'roll fans was the composition by Eddie and Hank Cochran that dated from around 1956.

"FOOTPRINTS IN THE SNOW"

Home recording of Buddy Holly with Bob Montgomery. Dates from '53

There are several home recordings of Buddy that pre-date the 'Holly In The Hills' material and on which his voice is adolescent. They are most definitely of academic interest only but do help chart the development of Buddy Holly from those earliest days right through to his final efforts in 1959 at age 22.

In the UK, the American, Johnny Duncan and his Blue Grass Boys seemed to tour British ballrooms endlessly on the back of this number and *"Last Train To San Fernando"*. Footprints has been a tune that has been handed down over the years and would have been staple material for country singers back in the '40s and '50s.

If -as has been said - Holly performed *"Gotta Travel On"* nightly during the final tour, who knows, he may also used the similar-styled *"Footprints in the Snow"*. Certainly older fans will be familiar with this song title and for this reason if little other, it ought to be released if and when a definitive collection of Holly material sees the light of day.

THE FOUR TEENS

Joe B Mauldin was the bassist with this local, Lubbock area rock'n'roll group, prior to moving on to join The Crickets.

Larry Welborn (see entry) also had a spell with The Four Teens who were little known outside their immediate area, although they did back singer Terry Noland for a spell. Also see entry TERRY NOLAND

FREDDIE AND THE DREAMERS

UK male vocal and instrumental group who shot to fame in 1963 on the back of the Northern beat boom.

Freddie Garrity (born 14th November 1940) the leader of this distinctive quintet and has been described as a Holly-look alike. If this is the case then surely a stronger claim could be made by Greek songstress, Nana Mouskouri?

Freddie used to feature *"It Doesn't Matter Anymore"* in his stage act - is still performing these days along with other hardy survivors of the '60s music scene.

March '58 - Holly with The Tanner Sisters during U.K. tour.

ALAN FREED

What a sad entry to write. It's absolutely certain that this legendary DJ, who did so much to promote rock'n'roll - and in its most ethnic form - died as an indirect result of his love of music. Every report indicates he died a broken man not long after the payola scandal had ripped the industry apart and led to him receiving a suspended prison sentence.

If payola was a painful episode for Freed, for Stan Freburg it was another excuse to parody the rock'n'roll scene in his wickedly deceptive way.

As to Holly and Freed there's a wonderful photo of the two with Larry Williams and the three are sporting bow ties. Considering rock'n'roll had such a rebellious image it is interesting to look back and to see the photographic evidence that most artists were smartly turned out. If one had to say something about the clothes it would be that often they were just 'different'.

There is an excellent interview with Holly by Alan Freed which took place at radio WNEX, New York. The interview appears in full on the MCA box set and there is a chilling section where Holly/Freed discuss planes crashing. Another section is mildly embarrassing with Freed trying to set up a humorous punch-line (Joe buy-us) but Buddy is far too impetuous and the joke is well and truly fluffed.

Alan Freed had a magnificent speaking voice and this has been captured on such albums as 'Alan Freed's Memory Lane' where he gives brief spoken intros to such legendary artist as The Moonglows and The Flamingos.

Often portrayed as a mere figurehead it is conveniently forgotten that he fronted a powerhouse big band that performed on tour bills and also made records.

Deservedly had a film made of his life 'American Hot Wax' (1978) which was a critical success. Freed was born 15th December 1922 and died 20th January 1965 of uraemia.

BOBBY FULLER

Founder, lead singer and guitarist with The Bobby Fuller Four who had two sizeable US hits in '66 on the Mustang label.

Bobby was heavily influenced by the sound of Buddy Holly and The Crickets and a few years ago a posthumous album, 'Memories of Buddy Holly' was issued on the Rockhouse label pulling together all Bobby Fuller's Holly-related material.

The death of Bobby Fuller at an early age has never been satisfactorily explained and it seems nonsensical to hint at a suicide verdict while his hit, *"Love's Made A Fool Of You"*, was still on the tail end of the US charts.

Whilst articles on Bobby Fuller have always stressed the links between the two artists Bobby Fuller was 23 and not the same age as Holly at the time of his untimely death as was reported. But Bobby certainly recorded a lot of material that has the spirit of Holly written all over it.

If one were looking for tenuous connections there are many. Bobby was a Texan from El Paso and his biggest hit was *"I Fought The Law"* which was penned by Sonny Curtis. Fuller's manager was Bob Keene (President of Mustang), who was the mentor and producer of Ritchie Valens. Norman Petty wrote to Fuller in early '66 and suggested that Bobby record in Clovis. Shall I go on or have you got the picture?

SNUFF GARRETT

Tommy 'Snuffy' Garrett has a musical CV too long to list in this publication. He started out as a DJ on a local Texas station in the '50s and is a true contemporary of Holly's, having been born in Dallas.

If you check out your musical collection you may find you have something Snuffy's been involved with, for example the series of instrumental albums - '50 guitars of Tommy Garrett' - was Snuff Garrett. He was musical supervisor on the 'Honky-tonk Man' film soundtrack which was just about the last thing Marty Robbins was involved in. He also recorded a quasi-classical album calling himself the 'Texas Opera Company'. Of course we mustn't forget that he produced the hit album 'Bobby Vee Meets The Crickets'.

In addition Snuffy was instrumental in helping get the Buddy Holly statue erected in Lubbock, Texas and fans owe him a debt of thanks for this. At the time of Buddy's death the two were planning to get together and form a music company called Taupe, which just happened to be the exact colour of Buddy's pink Cadillac Fleetwood.

Snuff Garrett is still active in the music business.

'GIANT'

Album

The name of the famous James Dean movie was shrewdly used by Norman Petty as the title for this 1969 album. In fact whilst additional Holly material had been discovered over the years this album was to be the last to include significant new stuff. Coming 10 years after Holly's death it was an exciting release and it is a surprise that the album crept into the charts for only one week.

The real criticism of the album has to be that the varied content - 1956 and 1959 demos are placed side by side - making for very uneven listening. Comments that the album was over - produced are not really valid although it remains disappointing that former Crickets were not asked to help on the overdubbing project.

JIMMY GILMER

Gilmer (vocalist - guitarist) teamed up with The Fireballs in 1961 and had a massive '63 hit with *"Sugar Shack"* on the Dot label.

Jimmy Gilmer used Norman Petty's Clovis studios to record his album 'Buddy's Buddy' in the early '60s. The title was a slight misnomer as the two artists never actually met and the Holly numbers on the album are all performed in a style which, while much removed from the originals, make for interesting listening.

See entry - THE FIREBALLS

LOU GIORDANO

Little known US artist who was born Louis Patsy Giordano on 23rd June 1929 and who died, age 40, on 22nd December 1969. As well as performing as Lou Giordano he also used the stage name, Lou Jordan. Had a single produced by Buddy and Phil Everly in late '58 for the Brunswick label which was released to good reviews in February '59 but which failed to chart.

The 'A' side of the disc was the Holly composition *"Stay Close To Me"* whilst the flip was a Phil Everly number *"Don'tcha Know"*. It is interesting to note that the backing 'girlie group' on the latter were, in fact, Holly, Phil Everly and Joey Villa of The Royal Teens. (It was probably Villa that introduced Giordano to Buddy and Phil).

Giordano had a lightweight voice and it is a pity Holly never recorded his own composition. If it was taped by Holly no sign of it has ever materialised. Incidentally, a superb version of *"Stay Close To Me"* was recorded by Mike Berry years later in which he incorporated a beautiful sequence of *"Words Of Love"*.

"GIRL ON MY MIND"

Second Nashville recording session at Bradley's Barn which included Jerry Allison on drums, 22nd Jul '56

A pedestrian ballad, it was written by Lubbock friend and bassist Don Guess who appeared on this and each of the 1956 Nashville sessions.

Never a hit it is interesting to note that it was released as both a 45 and 78 disc in the US during Holly's lifetime.

A few years back the Picks released the Holly vocal with their own dubbed backing vocals added. Whilst it helps somewhat it cannot totally transform what must remain - by Buddy Holly standards - a pretty mundane song. The criticism usually levied at the Holly recording is that he is trying to sing in too high a register a la Tony Williams of The Platters. Whatever the reason it is certainly one of Holly's less popular performances.

ARTHUR GODFREY

Big name in the States in the '50s primarily as a result of his regular Talent Scout shows.

It is on record that the Crickets failed an audition early '57 while waiting for one of their recordings to break out. Interestingly, around that time (January '57), Patsy Cline had appeared on the show which led to "*Walking After Midnight*" being a major hit record for her. The US version of Hughie Green, Godfrey also helped discover Guy Mitchell, Steve Lawrence and many other 'name' acts.

JOHN GOLDROSEN

Author of the trail-blazing US biography of Holly 'His Life And Music' in 1975.

He grew up in Worcester, Massachusetts, USA and graduated from Harvard in 1971. Shortly thereafter he gave up two years of his life to research the book. All Holly fans owe John a great debt as he was able to interview many important players in the Holly legend whilst they were still living. As of this writing is alive and well and runs his own bookstore in the state of Massachusetts. Of the many lay individuals who have helped promote Holly's posthumous career (Beecher/Griggs/Ingman, etc.) it was John Goldrosen, more than any other, who helped re-awaken America to the formidable talent of their native son.

"GONE"

Demo; recorded in Lubbock late '56/early '57

Buddy, with Jerry Allison, cut a demo version of this country number towards the end of '56. Earlier, he had completed three southern tours - as Buddy Holly and the Two Tones - and the line-ups featured mostly country acts. It is certain that this number would have been typical of the material featured at such concerts.

The song had been composed several years earlier by Smokey Rogers and Ferlin Husky had hits twice with the same number, under different names - the second time in early '57 when it became a major pop hit for him.

The Holly version - overdubbed as so much of that early stuff was - appeared first on the 'Showcase' album in 1964 - the album itself being a big seller and proving there was still a voracious appetite for new Holly material.

The song is simple but strikingly beautiful and Buddy's version, despite lasting only 69 seconds, is a good one given the garage-type recording circumstances which produced it. Undubbed earlier takes of "*Gone*" finally appeared on an 1986 album 'Something Special From Buddy Holly' on Rollercoaster which sadly is no longer in catalogue.

"GOOD ROCKIN TONIGHT"

Demo; recorded late '56 in Lubbock, Texas

First written and recorded by Roy Brown back in 1947 it was then covered by Wynonie Harris who had a pretty successful record with it in 1948 on the King label.

However, it was probably the Elvis performance on SUN 210 that Buddy first heard before proceeding to cut his own version at a practice session late '56. Never intended for release it finally came out on the 1969 'Giant' album with other unreleased product, all heavily overdubbed to give them a more commercial sound.

Those fans who wanted to hear how Holly sounded in a more raw and undiluted manner finally got to hear the truth when the undubbed recordings of this and other performances were released on the 1986 album 'Something Special From Buddy Holly'. Any fan not having these 'garage' recordings should do their level best to track down a copy of the deleted Rollercoaster album mentioned above which is essential listening.

"GOTTA GET YOU NEAR ME BLUES"

Buddy and Bob performance at Nesman Studio, Wichita Falls, Texas, Circa '54/'55

Long before Holly walked up the steps of the Pythian Temple in New York to undertake his final recording session with Coral he was cutting demos in a small local Texas studio at Wichita Falls. One of these was *"Gotta Get You Near Me Blues"*, written by Bob Montgomery and one of the most rhythmic of a batch of numbers they tried out in those early days.

Not recorded for commercial reasons it was nevertheless put out in the '60s with other similar performances on the 'Holly In The Hills' album. All the tracks are subject to some overdubbing, but just how much it is impossible to tell from these mono releases.

It would really be academic only to hear any of these Buddy and Bob performances in their original, undubbed format. But the songs do illustrate well the artists' strong country roots.

BILLY GRAMMER

Not a name that appears in every country reference book these days but that wasn't the case back in 1959 as, months earlier, he had a major hit with *"Gotta Travel On"*. Thereafter he became a regular on the Opry and was much in demand for many years.

It is documented that Holly performed *"Gotta Travel On"* during the final Winter Dance Party Tour and the lyrics, with hindsight, are sad but apt. The Billy Grammer disc entered the US charts in early December '58 for a fifteen week stay and it was natural for Buddy to perform this type of number on the bandstand.

Mentioning topical recordings, *"The Chipmunk Song"* by David Seville had entered the charts at the same time as the Grammer disc but whilst Buddy obviously never performed the number there was a connection which is discussed under the entry - *"SLIPPIN' & SLIDIN"*.

GRAND OLE OPRY/LOUISIANA HAYRIDE

Both showcases for Country music in the '50s and, of course, the Grand Ole Opry is around even today but more of a tourist attraction than as the mecca for country talent that it once was.

Buddy was certainly a fan of the Opry but would not have been a serious contender to perform on it. However artists such as Johnny Horton - only marginally more country - did appear and of course, so did Elvis Presley even if his performance was highly unsuccessful. A far better potential venue for Holly would have been the Louisiana Hayride at nearby Shreveport. Buddy and the boys did make an abortive attempt to appear following an introduction by Elvis but frustratingly it just didn't work out.

Interestingly, whilst we don't think of Holly in terms of country music it is a fact that he merits an entry in the majority of books concerning that genre that have appeared over the years.

LLOYD GREENFIELD

Acted as Buddy's agent in '58 and he claimed to be responsible for helping him with his later image. Certainly Holly had his teeth capped and his hair took on a more stylish look that year. Studying photos and film of the singer over a period of time a transition can certainly be picked up. But how much was from such advice we will probably never know.

At the time of the final New York Bruno photographic session, just prior to the final tour, the change of image was about complete. Sadly, the output from that photo shoot hardly got used during Buddy's lifetime but an example was to be used evocatively for the sleeve of 'The Buddy Holly Story' memorial album that was rush released in March of '59.

The author would welcome any further information on Lloyd Greenfield and on any entries in this publication where a major omission is thought to exist - see AFTERWORD.

BILL GRIGGS

Well known US super-fan of the late Buddy Holly.

Took up the torch in the '70s and organised a world-wide fan club which did a lot of good things. Bill even moved his home to Lubbock, Texas, doubling as a record dealer to finance his hobby.

In an exciting 10 year period lasting into the mid-eighties he was there to witness Buddy's statue being unveiled and to see Holly's life story turning up on celluloid. Bill helped to mastermind regular Lubbock conventions that acted as a magnet for fans from all over the world for very many years.

Not without his critics but only the deepest cynic would doubt his sincerity and none can challenge the contribution he has made in helping Holly's name live on.

DON GUESS

A contemporary of Buddy Holly from Lubbock, Texas whose main instrument was stand-up bass. Composed quite a lot of early material which was performed by Holly and Montgomery.

Appeared on many of the country 'Holly In The Hills' recordings and also toured with Buddy in '56 before the Crickets became established. Apart from Buddy himself, Don Guess was the only ever-present on all three of those Nashville sessions.

Don Guess seems such a feature of the early years that it is a shock not to see him listed as a 'Cricket' in a Crickets File publication listing 30 of them. If the file editor, John Firminger, reads this - think about it!

Don Guess passed away only a year or two ago.

GUITARS

A lengthy article appeared in the Guitar Player magazine back in June 1982 which listed details of all the many guitars owned by Buddy. The entry below is a very brief resume and anyone wishing to go further should try and seek out the back issue in question.

The first guitar that Buddy owned was a Harmony, made by a well-known Chicago-based firm who specialised in producing basic guitars for the mass market in the '50s. By the time he met J.I. he was playing a Gibson Les Paul 'Gold Top' which he possibly found a bit too heavy. Certainly he switched to a Fender Stratocaster pretty early on and it's that image that dominates the photos of Holly on the bandstand. (His most famous Strat was stolen from his station wagon in Canada whilst on tour and had to be quickly replaced).On the acoustic side Buddy initially used a Gibson J-45 and it is that instrument that he hand-tooled in leather which remains in the hands of brother Larry these days.

In 1958 Buddy designed his own hollow-bodied guitar with the help of Guild and there is speculation that he might have actually endorsed the particular model. That same year he also had a buying blitz picking up a Gibson J-200, a Guild F-50 Navarre (both acoustic) and two white Stratocasters.

An Epiphone (a Gibson related make) and a Gretsch have also been linked to Holly. Not a bad haul and that's not counting the famous Des O'Connor Hofner!

BILL HALEY AND THE COMETS

Born William John Clifton Haley on 6th July 1925, Bill Haley was in the forefront of rock'n'roll and it denigrates his memory when, as occasionally happens, he is talked of in unflattering terms.

Buddy Holly, with Bob Montgomery, appeared on a Comets bill in Lubbock, Texas back in October '55 and this ultimately led to Holly getting his first big chance to make a record. Whilst Buddy opened the bill in '55, in later years he appeared on other packages with Haley but very much as an equal.

Both artists had definite country roots but while Buddy's career was to be cut short Bill went on touring for decades before sadly dying prematurely at the age of 55, in Harlingen, Texas on 9th February 1981. His greatest music dates from his lengthy career with Decca although the output from his Essex days (pre-1954) and his later material (Warner Bros, Swedish Sonet etc.) was always eminently listenable.

BEN HALL

Ben Hall was born near Wichita Falls, Texas back in June 1924. Amongst his many talents are listed those of DJ, song-writer and publisher. He also fronted a band, Ben Hall and the Ramblers and was well known locally in the Lubbock area for many years, becoming involved in radio KDAV - see separate entry.

Buddy occasionally sat in with Ben Hall's group and eventual sought Ben's help in obtaining material to cut at his forthcoming Nashville recording session. *"Blue Days, Black Nights"* was the result and it has the distinction of being Buddy's first ever record release on US Decca 29854. Ben, with ace steel guitarist Weldon Myrick, also composed *"It's Not My Fault"* - one of the very best of Holly's earliest recordings which got deserved exposure as the flip of the posthumous hit, *"Bo Diddley"*.

Ben Hall has recorded his own versions of *"Blue Days, Black Nights"* and this and other material has recently been released by Rollercoaster records in this country.

JACK HANSEN

Producer of the first posthumous overdubbing session of Holly material which led to the single release of *"Peggy Sue Got Married"* and *"Crying, Waiting, Hoping"*. Thereafter was responsible for dubbed versions on the remaining four songs that Buddy had taped in his New York apartment in late '58.

Often referred to as the Jack Hansen combo (shades of Ernie Freeman) Hansen worked for Coral and had actually been the A&R man at the October session which produced *"True Love Ways"*.

The Hansen backings have often been criticised as being too heavy and by including a chorus on the tracks the end result is a bit overpowering. Unsurprisingly many fans favour the later, Tex-mex sound dubbed by Norman Petty which although instrumental only came nearer the 'feel' of the songs.

But the original Hansen versions are etched in our memories and for that reason will always retain a high level of popularity.

CHARLES HARDIN

Buddy Holly was christened Charles Hardin Holley and occasionally used the abbreviated format (Charles Hardin) on his composer credits.

GLEN D HARDIN

Former Cricket with a long pedigree which starts back in Lubbock, Texas where he grew up with Buddy Holly. Even as I write this (1994) Glen D Hardin has just finished collaborating with The Crickets on their latest album release (Rollercoaster CD 'Double Exposure').

His main instrument is piano/keyboard and he can often be glimpsed in footage of Elvis on stage during his Vegas years. Like some other Crickets his relationship with the group has been intermittent. In between times he has worked with a host of other artists although his spell with Elvis (1970-1976) was one of his longest involvements, before he left to join Emmylou Harris.

Incidentally, Glen D is not related to Holly in any way despite sharing the name, Hardin. Surprisingly, given his musical prowess, Glen's name seldom crops up in composer credits. Probably his best composition from Crickets days is the classic *"Teardrops Fall Like Rain"*.

Buddy Holly (with Fender) and member of Ronnie Keene's Orchestra, U.K. March '58.

"HAVE YOU EVER BEEN LONELY"

Practice tape; recorded in Lubbock late '56/early '57

A favourite of his mother's it was hardly surprising that Buddy attempted this number which had been quite a successful song for both Jaye P Morgan and for the Three Deuces in the USA. Back in England there were a host of cover versions but although the sheet music was a hit the actual records didn't chart.

The first release of Holly's recording was on the 1969 'Giant' album in an over-dubbed format. This gave the track a more commercial sound and had the twin benefit of transforming the original mono tape into a stereo release. (A benefit say some - but not all!)

Undubbed versions of all three takes of the song have been released on vinyl by Rollercoaster and despite the deteriorating condition of the tapes they are essential listening.

HAWAII

The night after performing on the Ed Sullivan TV Show (26th January 1958), the Crickets appeared on a stopover date at the Civic Auditorium, Honolulu, Hawaii on route to Australia.

This must have been a busy time for the boys as, a few days earlier, they also completed the *"Rave On"* session in New York. The troupe that appeared in Hawaii - not in the Union at that point - comprised of the Australian line-up of Jerry Lee, Paul Anka, Jodie Sands and The Crickets.

Some reports indicate that they put in a further appearance in Hawaii on the way back to the US and before embarking on The Big Gold Record Stars tour in Florida.

Some of the best colour photos of Buddy ever taken date from the Hawaiian trip courtesy of Norman Petty's camera.

"HEARTBEAT"

Recorded at Norman Petty Studios, Clovis, New Mexico, Jul/Aug '58. Joe B Mauldin (bass) replaced by George Atwood for this performance. Tommy Allsup - lead guitar

One of Buddy Holly's greatest solo performances and like *"Everyday"* its sustained impact over a period has totally eclipsed its original chart success. Barely a hit in the UK, it reached only No. 82 in the States. Buddy must have accepted the failure of this single and the follow up *"It Doesn't Matter Anymore"* had been released in the US coinciding with the start of the Winter Dance Party tour.

Composer credits for *"Heartbeat"* indicate Montgomery/Petty but it is generally accepted that Holly and Bob Montgomery collaborated on this number. The sound on this track was ahead of its time although in the States it was given the ugly label, 'Chalypso'.

Much covered over the years, actor and Holly-fan Nick Berry had a major hit with it in 1992, when it was used as the theme tune for a TV series of the same name. A sample of other versions include Humble Pie, Denny Laine, The Hollies, Bobby Vee, Skeeter Davis and others - but not The Crickets!

Buddy's own version has been released with overdubbed vocal licks by The Picks but it doesn't work well and the original recording remains the definitive one.

LARRY AND TRAVIS HOLLEY (AND OTHER FAMILY MEMBERS)

Older brothers Larry and Travis Holley have continued their support for Buddy's music over the years, eventually coming to terms with the personal tragedy of their younger brother's sudden cruel death at the age of 22.

It is Travis (born 1927) who is the most similar to Buddy in looks and build while Larry (born 1925) favours his mother's side in outward characteristics. Larry's working life has been spent running the family ceramic tile business which briefly employed Buddy and the boys while they awaited their big break. They even helped lay some tiles at Norman's Clovis studios in an effort to achieve better acoustics! Larry has also run a small independent record label (Cloud Nine) for several years now.

Sister Pat (born 1929) has also followed Buddy's career with much pride and recently appeared being interviewed on a TV documentary that featured 'the' Peggy Sue.

Carrying on the musical torch is Larry's daughter Sherry, who has cut several records and has just located to Nashville where she hopes to cut an album for the Goldwax label. She recently dropped the 'e' from her professional name and we can only hope that it brings her the success it bought to her famous uncle.

MR & MRS L O HOLLEY

Buddy had - still does - a wonderful supportive family who have always welcomed contact with fans and have been his greatest champion down the years.

Charles Hardin Holley was the youngest of four children born to Lawrence Odel Holley (Born 4th October 1901, Died 8th July 1985) and Mrs Ella Pauline Holley nee Drake (Born 29th August 1902, Died 20th May 1990). Brothers Travis and Larry and sister Patricia are alive and well at the time of writing.

Lawrence Holley had been born in Cooper, Texas before he moved to Dallas at a very early age. As was common in those far off days Mr Holley had a variety of diverse jobs; working as a carpenter, a tailor and even as a cook. By the time their youngest child was born the family were located at 1911 - 6th Street in Lubbock and although they were to move it was always within the confines of Lubbock.

Mr Holley senior led an active life until he was sidelined by a stroke during 1970. Earlier he had even helped produce and manage Niki Sullivan's career for a short time in the '60s. Lawrence and Ella Holley resided for many years after Buddy's death at their 56th street home where they continued to do all they could to promote and keep alive their son's name.

After his death, Mrs Holley lived on for several years, although becoming increasingly frail and passing on at the age of 87 after a stroke. Both parents emanated a lot of love and warmth and should not be confused with their celluloid counterparts that appeared in Holly's film bio-pic.

See also LARRY & TRAVIS HOLLEY entry.

BUDDY HOLLY STATUE

An 8′6″ heroic bronze sculpture was unveiled in Buddy's hometown, Lubbock, Texas, in 1980 close by the Civic Centre. It was sculpted by Grant Speed, a well-known American artist who was also born and raised in Texas. He used a unique style known as 'The half-breed' and visited Lubbock to see the work unveiled at a ceremony which brought together members of the original Crickets and Waylon Jennings amongst others. A limited number of miniature statuettes were also created and have become prized possessions of the lucky owners.

The main Holly statue initially stood somewhat forlornly in a grassy area without any adornment but in the later end of the '80s an attractive surround was built which incorporates a Walk of Fame. At a moving ceremony in 1986 former Crickets Jerry Allison, Joe B Mauldin, Niki Sullivan and Sonny Curtis were made inductees. Others honoured over the years read like a Who's Who of Texas musicians.

In recent years a monument to Holly and the other fallen stars was erected close to The Surf Ballroom in Clear Lake, Iowa, scene of their last concert appearance.

BUDDY HOLLY

Vital Statistics

Born Lubbock, Texas on 7th September 1936 to Ella and Lawrence Holley.

Buddy had dark brown hair, brown eyes and was 5′ 11 1/2″ tall and in UK parlance was approximately 10st 5lbs (145 pounds). He had poor vision and failed his physical for the armed services.

During his musical career he reportedly had a mild stomach ulcer and avoided alcohol. He was an occasional cigarette smoker - and also tried pipe smoking. Much the norm. for the lifestyle of the '50s.

Ancestry-wise he is believed to have English, Welsh and some Cherokee Indian blood.

Buddy was a practising Christian and a member of the Tabernacle Baptist Church in Lubbock, Texas. He is buried in Lubbock City Cemetery.

See VIOLIN and GUITARS entries.

MARIA ELENA HOLLY

(Born Santiago)

Buddy's widow. They married August '58 in a ceremony conducted at Holly's parents house in Lubbock, Texas. It is well-documented that Maria was a receptionist at the Southern Music Company in New York when the two met.

What is not so well-known is that they actually first met in early January '58 - a fact published when Maria was interviewed for the US teen '16' magazine in early '59. Whilst their relationship was short they had actually known each other over a year before the crash that claimed Buddy's life. Still a tragically brief period and it is obvious that she has never got over Holly's sudden death. (She miscarried in that same month of '59).

The two of them had temporarily based themselves in New York and had taken several career steps that would probably have borne fruit if fate had not intervened. One was to form a music publishing company, Maria Music and this and other plans, all fell apart in the early hours of 3rd February 1959.

"HOLLY HOP"

Practice tape ; recorded in Lubbock late '56/early '57

Buddy Holly never released an instrumental in his lifetime but two recordings have been issued posthumously *"Holly Hop"* and *"Honky Tonk"*. Both were recorded at the same practice session held close to Buddy's home on 19th Street Lubbock.

"Holly Hop" was an untitled instrumental and is probably the jam-type intro. number that Buddy used on his local radio appearances. This number and other material was passed to Norman Petty in the '60s and it was released, overdubbed on the 'Giant' album in 1969. (With no known composer credits, it was decided to put it down to Mrs Holley - so maybe it should be *"Holley Hop"*!).

The undubbed recording has been released subsequently on the Rollercoaster album, 'Something Special From Buddy Holly'.

THE HOLLIES

One of the very best groups that emerged at the time of the British beat explosion. Many think The Hollies choice of name is derived from that of Buddy Holly although alternatively the link is given as the name for a Christmas decoration. Certainly the styles of the groups (Hollies/Crickets) bear little similarity and the latter reason seems the more likely.

The Hollies did record a superb album 'Buddy Holly' for Polydor in 1980 and despite being TV-advertised it surprisingly failed to chart. Each Holly number is given an unusual treatment and they also refreshingly tackled lesser known material. Worth searching out - not just for completists.

"HONKY TONK"

Practice tape; recorded in Lubbock, Texas late '56/early '57

It's sometimes hard to remember just how massive the instrumental *"Honky Tonk"* was in the States. Part 1 and Part 2 of this number were in their Top 40 for close to six months in 1956. Unfortunately in the UK several versions sold well (Ernie Freeman/Bill Justis/Bill Doggett) and the impact was diluted.

The melody was written by members of Doggett's band and the number featured prominent sax by Clifford Scott. Holly's practice version substitutes guitar for sax and it works well - although never intended as a commercial release. It is infinitely better to listen to the undubbed version (the Rollercoaster LP again) where the whoops and shouts of Holly and Allison can be heard to better effect.

JOHNNY HORTON

Born Los Angeles 30th April 1925. Died Milano, Texas 5th November 1960

Buddy Holly and Johnny Horton had little in common except their Texan connections and that each was to die early in tragic circumstances. Although born on the West Coast, Horton was brought up in Tyler, Texas and was to become a regular performer on the LOUISIANA HAYRIDE - see separate entry.

Many of Johnny's distinctive compositions were based on historical events although his first million-seller *"Battle Of New Orleans"* was a traditional song which had been arranged by country artist, Jimmy Driftwood. He was enjoying his third major hit *"North to Alaska"* when he was killed in an auto accident returning from a show at the Skyline, in Austin, Texas. Hank Williams had coincidentally made his final appearance at the same venue (Johnny had also married Hank's widow).

Johnny Horton allegedly contacted Merle Kilgore from beyond the grave by getting the coded message 'The drummer is a rummer and cannot hold the beat' to him several years after his death.

"I FORGOT TO REMEMBER TO FORGET"

The Buddy Holly recording that never was. Not strictly true - as Buddy recorded a demo version for Radio KDAV of this classic number which was written by Charlie Feathers and Stan Kesler. Elvis' version was the flip of *"Mystery Train"* whilst Johnny Cash had it as the 'A' side of his single on SUN 321. No doubt it was included in live concert performances as Holly would have been very familiar with the song.

Sadly the demo by Buddy was destroyed - quite a disappointment. There have been other record titles associated with Holly, *"So Rare"* etc. please see entry - RUMOURS.

"I GAMBLED MY HEART"

Buddy and Bob performance at Nesman Studio, Wichita Falls, Texas. Circa '54/'55

A Buddy and Bob performance from early Radio KDAV days that formed part of the 'Holly In The Hills' album released in the mid-60s. Originally listed as a Bob Montgomery composition this was later corrected to Holly/Montgomery.

Very country indeed the track was overdubbed somewhat by Norman Petty prior to release and while the original version exists it is unlikely to get a release. (While for years there was unrest that the undubbed apartment tapes deserved release the same case could hardly be made for these earlier performances).

"I GUESS I WAS JUST A FOOL"

Demo recorded at Norman Petty Studios; Clovis, New Mexico, Feb/Apr '56

The odd track out of a batch of practice demos recorded by Buddy, Jerry, Sonny and Don Guess in the months between the January and July Nashville sessions. Odd because it was the only track not apparently overdubbed and is therefore only available in its original mono format.

A self-composition, the lyrics contain an emotional message and it tends to be a much overlooked recording. Possibly because the sound quality itself is less than top class. Incidentally, it was this composition that led to a search for a non-existent Holly recording *"I Tried To Forget"* - an alternate title for this song. See RUMOURS entry.

There are earlier demo versions of this number by Holly but whether they are capable of release is debatable.

"I'LL JUST PRETEND"

Home recording by Buddy Holley and Bob Montgomery, circa 1952

Buddy and school friend, Bob Montgomery recorded this hand-me-down melody during the early '50s. Bob sings lead while Buddy plays the mandolin and sings harmony.

This number (and *"Two Timin' Woman"*) are taken from practice tapes and were released as collectors items by Buddy's brother, Larry on his own local Holly House record label.

"I'M CHANGING ALL THOSE CHANGES"

Main version: second Nashville recording session at Bradley's Barn which inc. Jerry Allison on drums, 22nd Jul '56. See also text below re. Clovis version.

In the first few months of '59, following Holly's death, there were those in the UK who thought he'd sold out to rock'n'roll and turned to 'pop' with a capital P. Of course, we were in ignorance of those early Decca sessions 8 tracks of which belatedly got released in the shape of two bland-looking 7" Brunswick E.Ps. Fans were in for a shock - because these tracks included several rockabilly gems.

The self-composed number above was one such tune. *"Changing All Those Changes"* brings to mind the phraseology of *"I Forgot To Remember To Forget"* and drives along well with sharp lead guitar from Sonny Curtis.

An earlier, shorter version recorded at Clovis appeared on the posthumous album 'Reminiscing', as overdubbed by The Fireballs and made for a stereo release. Undubbed the track appeared on the 'For The First time Anywhere' album on MCA (1983) in mono.

A further 1955 demo is said to exist but has not surfaced as far as the writer is aware.

"I'M GONNA LOVE YOU TOO"

Recorded at Norman Petty Studios, Clovis, New Mexico on 1st Jul '57

The sheet music instructions to this say 'Moderato - with a solid rock'. A pretty good definition of this rhythmic number that could well have been used as an 'A' side. Instead it was the flip of *"Listen To Me"*, a sizeable hit for Buddy as a solo artist, in the UK, not in the US.

If Niki Sullivan - who was a Cricket at the time - didn't get to play on this recording session it is believed a real live insect fleetingly became the 4th Cricket! Turn up the volume on the fade-out and listen to the sound of a chirping cricket which is clearly audible.

Composer credits are listed as Joe B, Niki Sullivan and Norman Petty but Holly and Allison evidently had a big part in writing this powerful number. As well as double-tracking the harmony vocals Buddy also overdubbed a second guitar line on the finished recording.

Not a number that has routinely attracted cover versions. Blondie made a driving version of it when all things Debbie Harry were the rage.

"I'M GONNA SET MY FOOT DOWN"

Demo made at Norman Petty Studios, Clovis, New Mexico, Feb/Apr '56

Self penned number that Buddy performed as a demo while he was alternating between practising in Clovis and recording in Nashville. A driving performance it first appeared on the 'Reminiscing' album in 1963 with overdubbing courtesy of The Fireballs.

Twenty years later the unadulterated track was released, with others, on 'For The First Time Anywhere' album. Finally, The Picks have released Holly's vocal version with their own chirping background on a double album of Buddy's material.

"I'M LOOKIN' FOR SOMEONE TO LOVE"

Recorded as a demo along with *"That'll Be The Day"* on Feb 24th/25th '57, at the Norman Petty Studios, Clovis, New Mexico. See text below re. personnel.

This number was recorded a demo but subsequently assigned Master No. 102022 and released as the flip of the legendary number that catapulted the Crickets to the top of the hit parade.

Local musicians Gary and Ramona Tollett were used on backing vocals with Niki Sullivan whilst Larry Welborn played bass as Joe B Mauldin hadn't yet been enrolled in the group. Jerry was of course, on drums. Written by Holly, with a credit given to Norman Petty, the number has remained one of the most popular from the days of the Chirping Crickets and is featured on soundtrack albums of both the 'Buddy' stage show and the film biog.

Whilst occasionally studio chatter or out-takes exist of Holly's other recording sessions all we have from the lengthy session that produced this track and *"That'll Be The Day"* is 4 minutes 10 seconds of pure magic.

JOHN INGMAN

Unsung hero of the UK Buddy Holly scene. John has spent a great chunk of his adult life researching and compiling statistical information relating to Buddy Holly and the Texas music scene of that era, when not earning a living wage.

Hopefully, he will continue his passion for the Tex-mex sound for years to come.

INTERVIEWS WITH HOLLY/CRICKETS

Although several interviews have come to light over the years most of these are fairly lightweight in content as they date from the days when pop/rock was treated as ephemeral and not something that need analysing for posterity.

The best of these are included on the MCA box set that first came out in 1979. Also worthy of mention is a fairly lengthy interview with Canadian DJ Red Robinson that surfaced in the early '80s. More recently an interview with DJ Freeman Hoover has been released as part of a Crickets CD and makes for interesting listening. (Eddie Cochran is obviously present throughout).

It had been several years after Holly's death before the average UK fan got to hear his speaking voice. Prior to that the spoken lyrics in *"Listen To Me"* were about as near as we got. So it was interesting to eventually hear a clear Texan accent speaking in fond tones of his home town and with a lively sense of humour never far beneath the surface.

"IT DOESN'T MATTER ANYMORE"

With the Dick Jacobs Orchestra; recorded in stereo at Coral Records Studios, Pythian Temple, New York, 21st Oct '58

Posthumous UK No. 1 record for Buddy Holly in early '59. The track was composed by Paul Anka and the story goes that the number was only included on the session at the last minute. A quirk of fate that led to Dick Jacobs working up an inspired arrangement at short notice. Whilst a major hit in Britain it never hit the Top in Holly's homeland.

Listening to Paul Anka's original one is struck at the very different interpretation that the composer gives to the song. (Anka did in fact, later re-record the number much closer in style to the Holly version).

Holly's recording has stood up well to repeated playing over the years and still manages to sound fresh. The title is famous for being one of many ironic song titles that have been the kiss of death for certain unlucky performers. A quick sample includes *"Last Date"*/Mike Holliday, *"Welcome To My World"*/Jim Reeves, *"Three Steps To Heaven"*/Eddie Cochran and Hank Williams last big hit *"I'll Never Get Out Of This World Alive"*. Buddy Knox - probably protected by being born in Happy, Texas - tempted fate by recording *"I Think I'm Gonna Kill Myself"* but exercised commendable self-restraint.

Turning back to *"It Doesn't Matter Anymore"*, Johnny Worth had the Embassy (Woolworth's) cover that presumably sold a few copies - their recordings always being cheaper to purchase than the hit parade counterparts.

"IT'S NOT MY FAULT"

Demo made at Norman Petty Studios, Clovis, New Mexico Feb - Apr '56

A good country number written by Ben Hall and his one-time sideman Weldon Myrick that is short in duration (1 min. 48 sec.) but not in quality. One of many Holly performances that one feels, deserves greater exposure.

Overdubbed by The Fireballs the original release was on the 'Reminiscing' album. Has also been released undubbed and more recently The Picks have added backing vocals. The 21 tracks they overdubbed in 1984 are curiously uneven but this is one of the tunes that works quite well.

"IT'S SO EASY"

Recorded at Norman Petty Studios, Clovis, New Mexico on 25th May '58. Features lead guitar of Tommy Allsup

The last Crickets recording to feature Holly as lead singer it surprisingly flopped as a single in the States although we know Buddy and the boys did their best to promote it.

A Holly/Petty composition, royalties must have flowed in during '77 when Linda Ronstadt made it a Top 5 record Stateside.

The version by the Crickets includes heavy lead guitar that you can be forgiven for thinking is a steel instrument. This was the recording debut for the 'unknown' Cricket, guitarist Tommy Allsup, who was eventually to end up touring with Buddy.

Incidentally the current Crickets with lead singer Gordon Payne have just cut a punchy re-recording of the number with Sonny Curtis on lead guitar.

"IT'S TOO LATE"

Recorded at Norman Petty Studios, Clovis, New Mexico app. 19th Jul '57 inc. Niki Sullivan on guitar

While Buddy and the Two-Tones were out on the Sonny James tour, circa April 1956, Chuck Willis was in New York recording a session for Atlantic which included his own composition *"It's Too Late"*.

The Crickets cut their interpretation (very similar in style to the Willis version) in mid-'57 for inclusion, on their first album, 'The Chirping Crickets' that was released in the November.

The Picks added backing vocals at a separate recording session and it is this version that we have heard over the years. A tape without the Picks overdubs does exist but has not been issued commercially.

IVAN

Jerry Ivan Allison, co-founder of the Crickets with Buddy Holly, had a single released in '58 on the Coral label and it was put out using the pseudonym of 'Ivan', his middle name. The 'A' side, *"Real Wild Child"* has since become somewhat of a classic and Jerry's version holds up well against all-comers. The original recording of the song was by Johnny O'Keefe and had been styled *"Wild One"*-see entry under O'KEEFE.

Listening to the track it is surprising how identifiable Holly's voice is amongst the backing vocals. Whilst the record was good and a chart entry in the US, Jerry decided not to give up his day job - as a Cricket.

These days not only does Jerry do occasional backing vocals with The Crickets but has even recorded lead vocals - not surprisingly in a very laid back manner. See also entries under ALLISON and PEGGY SUE GARRON.

DICK JACOBS

Dick Jacobs was A&R Director with Coral Records, a sub-division of Decca, which was formed in 1949. Buddy eventually signed for Coral, the irony being that he had originally signed for Decca and his contract had as good as lapsed when early recordings failed to lift off. Holly, along with the Johnny Burnette Trio, remained with Coral although the label only really dabbled with rock'n'roll and made no real attempt to build a roster of artists. (Although Bill Haley was with Brunswick - part of the same stable).

Jacobs produced both the *"Early In The Morning"* session and the final New York session at the Pythian Temple which included *"True Love Ways"* and three other recordings. It is quite possible that Dick Jacobs would have continued to work with Holly from time to time as both were contracted to Coral.

Several years back Dick was allegedly stabbed by his wife and sustained severe injuries, but has since made a full recovery.

Buddy, Joe B., and Jerry backstage during UK tour March '58.

WAYLON JENNINGS

Waylon was born just down the road from Lubbock at Littlefield in Texas on 15th June 1937, just a year younger than his friend and contemporary Buddy Holly. They had met first around 1954 when both had appeared on the 'Sunday Dance Party' on KDAV radio.

Eventually Waylon got to work as a DJ on radio KLLL in Lubbock and after he had made it, Buddy would often drop in at the station and even took time to record jingles to the tunes of *"Everyday"* and *"Peggy Sue"*, advertising the station. Shortly thereafter Holly helped produce Waylon's first attempt at recording on the session that included celebrated saxophonist, King Curtis. The Cajun standard *"Jole Blon"*, backed with *"When Sin Stops"* by Waylon was not released till May '59 (US Brunswick 55130) and despite reasonable reviews it sunk without trace. Probably not helped by the fact that following Holly's death Waylon had quit the music business and was not in the mood to promote the single.

Whilst he toured with Buddy, but didn't officially record with him, Waylon still features in Holly discography having helped to compose *"You're the One"* and performed hand claps on the informal session at the station where the number was taped.

Waylon Jennings recorded a dramatic tribute-style record *"The Stage"* in the '60s and this is hard to locate these days. Later, a much more subtle tribute, *"Old Friend"* was recorded which was about Buddy by insinuation. (Holly's name is not actually mentioned in the lyrics, but the message is crystal clear).

There is a classic few seconds of colour footage of the Crickets circa. 1957 and this and a colour clip of Buddy and Waylon together at KLLL on Waylon's authorised video biography a year or two ago. In fact there is a long opening sequence in which Waylon reminisces about his early Lubbock days and his association with Buddy who was very much his mentor.

To bring the Holly/Jennings link up to date, until a few years ago Gordon Payne, current lead vocalist with The Crickets was a member of Waylon's touring band.

JINGLES

Promotional jingles by recording artists were the norm in the '50s , achieving the dual purpose of boosting an artists current record release , whilst at the same time bringing kudos to the radio station whose airwaves were being used.

In the fall of '58 Holly sang brief snatches of both *"Everyday"* and *"Peggy Sue"* in extolling the merits of radio KLLL. The jingles have been circulating amongst fans for years and a legitimate release on record is well overdue. (They are on a Live Gold album released in the US in 1991).

Buddy and the boys had also recorded 'thank you's" to Murray Deutch and Bob Theile to the tune of the Crickets first hit record - see entry under *"THAT'LL BE THE DAY"*.

BEN JOHNSON

Lubbock pastor who officiated at Buddy and Maria's August 1958 ceremony. Buddy was a firm Baptist and often attended his local church. Prior to his death he tithed monies from his earnings which is a far cry from earlier days when he was hard up and for a short period only just kept up with his car payments.

GEORGE JONES

Famous, much revered country artist, who could be termed a singer's singer as many artists own something to George's delivery. His voice sounds 'lived in' and given his life story this is hardly surprising.

George Jones was born 1931 in Saratoga, Texas and he and Buddy often toured on bills together during 1956 and as fellow Texans, one assumes they got on pretty well. Jones himself was on a rockabilly kick in those days and had one or two good-sized hits for the Starday label.

A more tangible link was that between George Jones and The Big Bopper. Both were Mercury artists and George had country success with a string of J P Richardson compositions, most noticeably *"Beggar To A King"*, *"Running Bear"* and *"White Lightning"*.

MALCOLM JONES

The late lamented Malcolm Jones wrote the comprehensive sleeve notes on the World Records box set of Holly recordings around 20 years ago. Later he collaborated with John Beecher on the MCA box set which - to date - remains the definitive collection. (First out in 1979 it needs revising!).

He spent most of his working life in and around the record business setting up the HARVEST label for EMI and the small independent, Fly Records, in 1970. A meticulous individual he did not always get the recognition he deserved but is thought of with gratitude by Holly fans.

Malcolm died on 17th February 1990.

RADIO KDAV & KLLL

The main radio station operating out of Lubbock in the early '50s was KSEL which comprised a mainly pop format. Around 1953 Ben Hall, Hipockets Duncan and Dave Stone - all associated with the station - got together to form radio KDAV which was quite certainly one of the first stations to operate an all-country format. It was KDAV that was to run a popular Sunday Party feature on which Holly and Bob Montgomery were to make regular appearances. (Much of the 'Holly In The Hills' material is culled from tapes of their performances).

In 1958 another Lubbock station (KLLL) was taken over by the Corbin brothers (see separate entry under CORBIN) and also changed to an all-country format. It was on K triple-L, as it was known, that Waylon Jennings went to work as a DJ although he had known Holly from a few years previous.

A brief segment of colour film exists showing both Jennings and Holly together in the radio station circa '57. Holly was to 'record' *"You're The One"* with Waylon at KLLL and this was subsequently given a release several years after Holly's death.

To round off this section please see comments under JINGLES heading.

BUDDY KNOX

Born three years before Holly (14th April 1933) in Happy, Texas, he cut the original of his big hit *"Party Doll"* at Norman Petty's Clovis, New Mexico studios in 1957.

Certainly Knox, with his group The Rhythm Orchids, were friends and acquaintances of Buddy and the boys and Holly is thought to have played guitar on at least one of Buddy Knox's '58 sessions. (There had been an element of competition with Buddy Knox managing to get his big break via Roulette a few months before Holly).

Buddy Knox has a light and pleasing voice and has made many good records, while never having been at the cutting edge of rock'n'roll. Has lived during more recent years in Canada and has intermittently toured the UK over the years.

Tempted fate by recording *"I Think I'm Gonna Kill Myself"* at a session which included members of the Crickets. Whilst Bo Diddley invented the riff that became rather famous and carries his name, Knox created his own distinctive rhythm pattern that was seldom copied but is classic in its own way.

TREVOR LAILEY

Currently runs the British Buddy Holly Society which he co-founded with Ray Needham back in 1981.

Trevor is an unassuming individual but has helped promote Holly's name in a variety of ways over the years. Gave helpful advice at the outset when the decision was made to launch the stage musical, *"Buddy"*.

DENNY LAINE

Was a member of Wings when he recorded a solo LP, 'Holly Days' aided and abetted by his boss Paul McCartney, who produced the album and was partly responsible for the concept. The ten tracks are highly listenable and particularly welcome is the inclusion of some of the less well-known numbers; *"Lonesome Tears"*, *"Look at Me"* etc.

The trend for other artists to record Holly material continues to the present day and recently (1993) the Lemonheads - as contemporary as you can get - recorded *"Learning The Game"*.

"LAST NIGHT"

Recorded at Norman Petty's Clovis, New Mexico studios, 12th Mar '57. Incs. Niki Sullivan on guitar

A fortnight after the legendary session which produced *"That'll Be The Day"* a further session was held at Clovis but this time the group comprised of the soon-to-be-famous quartet of Holly/Allison/Mauldin and Sullivan,. It was at this session that *"Maybe Baby"* was attempted using a different rhythm to the more famous recording made whilst on the road at the Tinker Airforce base, Oklahoma City.

"Last Night" was written by Joe B for The Four Teens, the group that Mauldin had left to join The Crickets. Part of the deal in allowing this number to be recorded was adding Norman's name to the composer credits. Shortly afterwards The Picks recorded the backing vocals and the track was one of twelve which formed one of the greatest albums ever released: 'The Chirping Crickets'.(In 1987 an international panel listed their all-time 100 albums and Chirping was placed No. 78. If that sounds low, well 'Purple Rain'/Prince and 'Imagine'/John Lennon, were lower!).

Surprisingly both *"Oh Boy!"* and *"Last Night"* have been released undubbed, i.e. ex-Picks, but only on bootleg style albums. MCA are presumably biding their time.

"LEARNING THE GAME"

Taped at Holly's New York flat, 17th December 1958

"Learning The Game" was the last of six songs that Buddy had written and experimented with on his recorder in their Greenwich Village flat during the run-up to Christmas '58. Shortly after he and Maria flew to Lubbock for the festivities before travelling back to New York at the year end. In January '59 he recorded further home-produced material but all feature songs that he had known since his early rock'n'roll days and they cannot touch the creative output of the previous month.

Holly's rendition of *"Learning The Game"* heavily overdubbed by Jack Hansen of Coral was released as a UK single in October 1960 and was a minor Top 40 hit. All six of Holly's compositions were included on the follow-up memorial album ('Buddy Holly Story, Vol. 2') which joined 'The Buddy Holly Story' in the UK album charts.

"Learning The Game" is a track which is particularly popular with discerning Holly fans and while the lyrics are not meant to be analysed the song title could and should be used as a comment on life. I would use the word 'credo' if it didn't have religious overtones.

All three versions (undubbed/Hansen and Petty overdubs) are available via the MCA boxed set.

JERRY LEE LEWIS

Celebrated rocker from Ferriday, Louisiana who is one of the true Greats of the music business. Still able to mesmerise audiences though nearly 60 (born 20th September 1935) and long may that continue. Effortlessly manages to balance a rock and country career without alienating fans. Remember, no version of any song is definitive until Jerry has cut it!

The paths of Jerry Lee and Buddy crossed from time to time during the '50s and it is disappointing that genuine quotes by Jerry about Buddy are few and far between. But there are two excellent photos of them both together, which (naturally) feature The Killer seated at the piano. One of these - used on the reverse of a Lewis album cover - has Buddy playing his fender and is a classic snap of the period.

A tape of Jerry and Buddy exists from late February 1958 singing *"Drown In My Own Tears"* and *"Hallelujah, I Love Her So"*. Rumour has it the quality is quite good. Hopefully these recordings will one day see the light of day.

Of course, The Crickets and Jerry Lee were both headliners on the Australian tour that had started in Sydney during the January and it is also disappointing that a minimal amount of 'memorabilia' (photos/interviews etc.) have survived from that visit - albeit the tour was a brief one.

"LISTEN TO ME"

Recorded at Norman Petty studios, between 29th June and 1st July '57. Group - Buddy/Jerry/Joe with Holly double-tracking vocals/guitar

Quite incredible to look back and realise that this classic Holly solo recording was NOT a US hit. It was not even released there as an 'A' side - that honour went to *"I'm Gonna Love You Too"*., which also failed to chart.

Written by Buddy (as Charles Hardin) and with composer credits shared with Norman Petty, it is one of the earliest attempts by any artist to dual-track and comes off spectacularly well. Another unusual feature of the track was a rather dead-pan spoken segment mid-way through. No trace of any Texan accent either.

"Listen To Me" was a major hit in the UK and a standout track on his first solo Coral LP. Later re-issues of that album were actually entitled 'Listen To Me' - a command most fans have happily obeyed ever since.

"LITTLE BABY"

Recorded at Norman Petty Studios, Clovis, New Mexico, 17th December 1957. The trio of Buddy, Jerry and Joe, were supplemented by C W Kendall Jnr., Pno

Very much an album track, part-written by the pianist on the session, C. W. Kendall junior, who normally lined up as part of The Big Beats - a Dallas group fronted at one stage by Trini Lopez.

Musically the number has a very unusual structure and it is hardly surprising that it has seldom attracted covers. Jimmy Gilmer did put out a very different interpretation on his album 'Buddy's Buddy'.

The Holly version was issued during his lifetime on his first solo album and posthumously, was included on the second volume of the 'Story' album to make up the standard twelve tracks. (Other unreleased material had not been fully collected together at that point).

"LONESOME TEARS"

Recorded at Norman Petty Studios, Clovis, New Mexico on 25th May 1958. Features lead guitar of Tommy Allsup

Both sides of the Crickets follow up to *"Think It Over"* were recorded at the same May '58 session and backing vocals were added by the Roses. It failed to chart and coincidentally, happens to have been the last Crickets single release during Holly's lifetime.

Both melody and lyrics were written by Holly and despite the fact that it is an attractive number, it has had hardly any exposure. For years it was not available on album in the UK - remedied by the release of the 'Remember' album in '71.

"LOOK AT ME"

Recorded at Norman Petty's Clovis, New Mexico Studios, Dec '57

Recorded just after Niki Sullivan left the group , this heavily piano-based number was used on Holly's first solo album and was not considered obvious single material . But it did get a posthumous release on 45 rpm in this country late 1961 when it was used as the follow up single to *"You're so Square"* but met with little success.

The UK Coral single Q 72445 is worth seeking out as it has been run through an echo chamber and is noticeably *"different"* to the original master recording for this reason.

The number was part composed by Buddy Holly and whilst his songbook has been heavily plundered over the years this is one of those tracks that gets overlooked.

TRINI LOPEZ

In the early '60s, just before Trini Lopez hit the big time, he looked poised to join The Crickets as lead vocalist but it never got to happen. (Story was that the Crickets were sidelined for several months after J.I. broke a bone and at the same time things started happened for Trini.)

Trini Lopez is usually labelled a Chicano artist - along with Valens, Romero, etc. - and was born on 15th May 1937, in Dallas, Texas, where he performed on the local scene from an early age.

Holly and Lopez were certainly contemporaries with Lopez heading a Dallas group called the Big Beats who also used Norman Petty's studios around '57/'58. If Trini had become involved with The Crickets the 'Tex-mex sound' label first used in Holly's day would have surely been revived - even if the phrase is a relatively meaningless one.

LOUISIANA HAYRIDE

See joint entry with GRAND OLE OPRY.

"LOVE IS STRANGE"

Taped at Holly's New York flat, Jan '59

One of a batch of tunes Buddy left on tape at his New York flat just before embarking on the final tour. Of the five different numbers, two were released in 1963 ('Reminiscing' LP) while the remainder had to await the release of the 'Giant' album in '69.

The song was part-written by Mickey Baker, one half of the Mickey and Sylvia duo, who had a sizeble '57 US hit with their version. Ten years later Peaches and Herb took it back into the charts while in the UK The Everly Brothers did a very powerful interpretation that got to No. 11. Strangely, it virtually marked the end of their hits for the Warner Brothers label.

Holly's version - issued as a single to coincide with the release of the 'Giant' album - failed to chart which, in retrospect, was surprising. The shortened, undubbed recording eventually appeared on the MCA box set. (The dubbed version has Buddy's short vocals used twice to produce a full-length commercial release).

Although official composer credits are Baker/Ethel Smith it has been rumoured over the years that it was co-written by Bo Diddley, Ethel Smith being the name of Bo's wife. In fact Chess had turned down Bo's original composition, *"Paradise"*, on which Mickey and Sylvia had based their number. *"Love Is Strange"* was later to figure in a lawsuit in connection with the Billy Stewart number *"Billy's Blues"*. The Bear family CD *"Love Is Strange"*, Mickey and Sylvia details all the convolutions and is highly recommended.

"LOVE ME"

First Nashville recording session at Bradley's Barn, 26th January 1956

Buddy's first real commercial attempt at recording and it duly became the flip of his initial Decca 45 disc, *"Blue Days, Black Nights"* in '56. The number was written by Buddy in collaboration with local songwriter, Sue Parrish and he had performed it several weeks earlier at a demo session in Wichita Falls. (This earlier more ragged attempt has been released over the years on bootleg-type albums.)

The composition itself is not a memorable one and has not attracted cover versions. The Buddy Holly Nashville recording was re-issued in 1984 with vocal embellishments by The Picks.

"LOVE'S MADE A FOOL OF YOU"

Recorded at Norman Petty's Clovis, New Mexico studios, Jul/Aug '58. Tommy Allsup, lead guitar. Jerry and Joe replaced by session men.

One of Holly's greatest recordings, it was put down as a demo for the Everlys in Norman Petty's studios during the summer of '58. Thereafter it remained unissued because of legalities to do with Holly's estate and it only turned up six years later as part of the 'Showcase' album. Months later, chosen as a single, it crept into the Top 40.

Discographical details show the recording as being overdubbed. In fact recently an undubbed version - which seems to lack hand claps only - was released on a European album and should be sought out by all genuine collectors.

The sheet music for this Holly composition reads 'moderately with a strong beat' which seems a reasonable instruction but Buddy's dual-tracked vocal is quite gentle. The feeling that this was recorded as a demo for the Everlys is quite striking.

Strong rock'n'roll versions of the number - making it almost seem a different composition - were hits for the Bobby Fuller Four, Matchbox and the post-Holly Crickets themselves.

LUBBOCK, TEXAS

Birth place of Charles Hardin Holley which is described as the Hub City of the South Plains. certainly Lubbock is far bigger in size these days than it was during Holly's brief lifetime. One thing is for sure - anyone visiting that part of Texas gets the feeling that the country is still new and evolving.

Consult the guide book and you learn that Texas was an independent Republic, with its own flag, as late as 1845. That's yesterday to us in the UK - or last week to avoid exaggeration.

One of the nicest aspects of the Holly story is that he was always very proud of his roots and never made any attempt to distance himself from Lubbock, even though temporarily he had based himself in New York. Signs were that he was going to gravitate back to Texas and make that his main base.

For many years there was little recognition of Holly's achievements in his home town but these days the Civic authorities certainly acknowledge their famous son, whose family still mainly live in and around Lubbock.

ROD LUCIER

No other details to hand, but Rod Lucier was the road manager on the final 1959 Winter Dance Party Tour.

ROBIN LUKE

US singer who was somewhat of a one-hit wonder and who has seldom been heard of since. But the hit *"Susie Darlin'"* was a monster (peaking at No. 5 in Billboard) and it became one of the best Summer hits of that year (1958).

Several years back Robin Luke was located (he was a doctor practising his vocation in Hawaii) and interviewed about his involvement with Buddy Holly. It seems the two met up on some tour and Holly spent virtually a complete day showing Robin Luke his guitar style and passing on quite a lesson in the art of playing that instrument.

Coincidentally *"Susie Darlin'"* was very much influenced by Holly and it did lead to Luke being termed a copyist, something, one feels, he would not deny.

"MAILMAN SEND ME NO MORE BLUE'S"

Recorded at Norman Petty Studios, Clovis, New Mexico on 8th April 1957. Buddy, Jerry, Joe B plus Vi Petty, piano

Apart from having 'blues' in the title the sheet music exhorts any would-be musician to adopt a blues beat on this unusual number. Partly written by Bob Thiele (see separate entry) under the non-de-plume Stanley Clayton it was pushed to Buddy who cut it early in '57. It subsequently came out in the US as the 'B' side of the *"Words of Love"* single, but the record flopped. Whether for this reason or not it didn't get a single release here at the time.

'50s balladeer Don Cornell - who hit No. 1 in the UK with *"Hold My Hand"* - was also on Coral Records and cut his own interpretation. Curiously his version was released, both here and in the US but it didn't manage to revive his flagging chart career.

Holly's UK single *"Look At Me"* with *"Mailman"* as the flip was a posthumous release but didn't chart. But it is quite collectable as both sides of the single had a strong dose of 'echo' added to it. Presumably to give it a more commercial sound.

JOE B MAULDIN

Joe Benson Mauldin, bass player with The Crickets was born 8th July 1939 and joined the group early in 1957 - just after *"That'll Be The Day"* was recorded. He was a mainstay in The Crickets for the next 18 months until the split with Buddy (probably temporary only) occurred. Joe B had previously played bass with the Four Teens, a Lubbock group who featured Terry Noland as their lead singer.

Most recognisable playing stand-up bass, photos came to light several years back showing him backing Buddy but using an electric bass on stage. This came as a belated shock to UK fans familiar with the group from the days of the '58 British tour. (Incidentally, if The Crickets had not performed in Cardiff on 24th March then it would have been a tour of England only).

As with the Jerry Allison entry Joe B's name is synonymous with that of Holly and a lengthy CV is not appropriate here. For any readers not switched on - subscribe to The Crickets File and get 'with it'.

Joe is still performing and recording with The Crickets (Gordon Payne/Jerry/Joe) and looks in good shape. He has even helped out on vocals occasionally in recent times. He spoke eloquently of his association with Holly on the definitive Arena television documentary of Buddy's life.

"MAYBE BABY"

Hit version recorded on the road, Oklahoma City, late Sept '57, The Crickets were a quartet at that time

Released on the eve of the Crickets March '58 UK tour, the single rocketed up the charts and peaked at No. 4, staying in the hit parade close to three months. Apparently Mrs Holley (mother) had some input into the lyrics, although the number is credited to Holly and Petty.

The hit version has a drum pattern similar to the Richard Penniman hit *"Lucille"* and the overall sound, including Picks overdubbed backing vocals, is unique. Six months earlier the quartet had cut a version of the same song, using a totally different rhythmic pattern and not surprisingly it was held back from release.

It was not until 1966 that, quite unheralded, the 'alternate' version was released in the UK. It received no promotion and failed to chart. (What was little known at the time was that this 'new' version was itself heavily overdubbed; virtually obscuring Niki Sullivan's harmony vocals).

The Crickets performed a live version of *"Maybe Baby"* on Off The Record in '58 and an audio tape of this exists. It is to be hoped it is one day given an official release.

PAUL McCARTNEY

Former Beatle, born June 1942 who has never denied his indebtedness to Buddy Holly from his earliest, formative years when growing up in Liverpool. The entry under 'Buddy Holly' in the Ultimate Beatles Encyclopaedia/Virgin Press makes this clear and should be read.

In the Seventies McCartney bought the Nor Va Jak music catalogue form Norman Petty which comprised titles ranging from *"An Empty Cup"* to *"You've Got Love"*. One assumes that move was a good one on both an emotional as well as on a business level. Spasmodically, since 1976, McCartney has promoted a Buddy Holly Week each September, celebrating the anniversary of Holly's birth (7th September) in a host of different ways.

There is no doubt that McCartney's involvement with the memory of Buddy Holly is quite genuine. In 1986 McCartney's company co-produced the definitive film biography of Holly's life - a formidable project - whilst just a few years ago McCartney both produced and played on the single *"T-shirt"* for the still-active Crickets group.

ECHO McGUIRE

Girl friend of Buddy during his High School years in Lubbock. They first started dating soon after they met at the age of 15. Although both came from a church-going background , Echo was apparently much more conservative than Buddy and while she didn't attempt to stop his musical ambitions, she gradually became less than comfortable with her role in his life.

The relationship continued for a while, even after she began to attend a Christian college in Abilene around 1955 and they kept in contact for a year or two thereafter. She finally got married to a college classmate and settled down to what was probably routine domestic bliss.

In the film biography of Holly's life he leaves his Lubbock girlfriend (presumably Echo) explaining his decision to her by saying those immortal words *"Just tell them bula-bula."*

DON McLEAN

See *"AMERICAN PIE"* entry.

JOE MEEK

Born Robert George Meek in Newent, Gloucester in 1929, Joe Meek became an avant-garde record producer in the late '50s and was responsible for some of the most innovative sounds in British pop music.

His biggest hit was with the Tornados in *"Telstar"* although his association with John Leyton was equally impressive. In 1961 he produced the classic *"Tribute to Buddy Holly"* by Mike Berry, that was leased to HMV and became a minor hit. The number was written by the enigmatic Geoff Goddard, who claimed, controversially, to have made spiritual contact with Holly.

Eventually Joe's career went into a downward spiral and he committed suicide in bizarre circumstances on 3rd February 1967, the 8th anniversary of Holly's death.

"MEMORIES"

Buddy and Bob performance at radio station KDAV. Circa '54/'55

One of the batch of early country-style performances that dates from Buddy and Bob days and which was eventually released in the '60s via the 'Holly In The Hills' album. *"Memories"* was one of a handful of tracks that did not get an official US release until the box-set came out there in 1981.

"Memories" was attributed to Bob Montgomery and the recording we are familiar with includes some unspecified overdubbing on it.

MICKEY AND SYLVIA

Holly was a big fan of this duo, who had a million-seller on Groove in 1957 with *"Love Is Strange"*. The group comprised of McHouston 'Mickey' Baker (Born 15th October 1925) and Sylvia Robinson (born 6th March 1936) who first met in 1955 and had a productive partnership that remained active for 10 years. Incidentally both had solo recording careers before and after their days as a duo.

Buddy Holly left two Mickey Baker compositions (they were also Mickey and Sylvia recordings) on tape in his New York flat, these being *"Love Is Strange"* and *"Dearest"*. The latter is surely one of Holly's best vocals and an alternative performance has surfaced on the bootleg-style Apartment Tapes album.

Often called Mickey 'guitar' Baker he remains a proficient guitarist up to present time, having moved from the pop realm to the jazz arena.

"MIDNIGHT SHIFT"

First Nashville recording session at Bradley's Barn 26th January 1956

Excellent rockabilly track from Holly's first Decca session under Owen Bradley. Didn't get a US single release at the time but was the posthumous follow up on Brunswick to *"It Doesn't Matter Anymore"* in the UK and made the charts in the summer of '59.

Principal composer was 'Earl Lee', a pseudonym for Luke McDaniel. Despite memorable lyrics and a good melody the track has seldom attracted cover versions although Sonny (Curtis) has perennially featured it in his act and committed it to wax on a recent Ritz album.

There is a version of the Holly recording overdubbed by the Picks that came out a few years ago. Opinions vary amongst fans of the wisdom of the project which involved 21 dubbed recordings in all - see entry THE PICKS.

GARY MILLER

Little known UK balladeer who had numerous single releases to his name in the '50s and '60s but who is probably best remembered for his cover of *"The Story Of My Life"* - Michael Holliday having the hit version.

In 1958 appeared on the same UK tour bill as the Crickets and there are pictures extant of Miller with Holly from those days. Rather strangely, released a Pye single *"Maria Elena"* in '63 which was not an allusion to Buddy's widow but rather a vocal version of the instrumental hit by 'Los Indios Tabajaros'.

Gary Miller died suddenly from natural causes in the mid-sixties when only in his '40s. His recording material is seldom re-issued these days which seems a harsh judgement on a very able artist.

MITCH MILLER

Mitch Miller, his orchestra and chorus, were a big success during the '50s and even had a No. 1 disc, *"The Yellow Rose Of Texas"* for Columbia in 1955. In addition Miller was A&R man for the label and it was hardly surprising for Norman Petty (whose Trio were signed to the label) to contact him and seek to place *"That'll Be The Day"* with Columbia. The label were not exactly famous for its roster of rock'n'roll artists and Mitch Miller was to pass up his chance to sign the group.

Shortly thereafter Murray Deutch and Bob Thiele entered the picture and we have to accept that everything that happened was for the best.

Mitch Miller retired from the active music business many years ago.

"MODERN DON JUAN"

Final Nashville recording session at Bradley's Barn. 15th Nov 1956, Backing musicians - session men - see below

This track formed the 'A' side of Buddy's second US Decca single but it failed to make any impact. Perhaps being released on Christmas Eve (1956) didn't help.

The number was written by Lubbock friends Jack Neal and Don Guess. The latter actually played bass on the session and was the only musician there who was not part of the Nashville set-up. The recording features a prominent saxophone, usually believed to be that of the legendary Boots Randolph. Perhaps the most surprising fact about the recording is that it's supposedly 'Take 76'! (Whilst loyal fans adore out-takes we must give thanks that each take from Number 1 to 75 no longer exist).

The recording is also available belatedly overdubbed by The Picks.

"MONA"

Rehearsal at Norman Petty Studios, Clovis, New Mexico probably late '57

It is only in the last few years that nearly 10 minutes of tape was discovered of Buddy, Jerry and Joe rehearsing this famous Bo Diddley number. If the session had been completed to everybody's satisfaction the track could well have ended up on Holly's first solo album , which was in course of preparation at that time. Whilst Holly's vocals are off-mike the bonus is to hear some excellent practice guitar. Jerry Allison is also heard strumming during the lengthy work-out.

These rehearsals have been released on bootleg-type albums in recent years, along with similar work-outs of *"Fools Paradise"*, *"Think It Over"* and *"Take Your Time"*.

"Mona" was eventually taken high into the charts in 1990, courtesy of Australian soap star, Craig McLachlan.

BOB MONTGOMERY

Buddy Holly and Bob Montgomery were firm friends from early school days in Lubbock, Texas, although Bob himself was born in Lamasas several hundred miles away.

They teamed up as a duo (see BUDDY AND BOB entry) and during '54/'55 cut several demo-type recordings, either at nearby Nesman Studio, Wichita Falls or at radio KDAV where they performed weekly on the Sunday Party. Although heavily influenced by country artists such as Hank Williams and Bill Monroe, the boys were not just parodists and in fact performed many of their own compositions. It is interesting to listen to these early 'country' attempts but frustrating that overdubbing robs them of some of their authentic sound.

Although Bob travelled to Nashville when Buddy got his first break, he did not perform on any of the recordings. Bob Montgomery has since become a highly respected figure in country music and has had success up to this day. Back in the '60s and '70s he produced major hits for Bobby Goldsboro, whilst moving onto the '80s he has produced hits for country stars; Janie Frickie and Razzy Bailey. He has been based in Nashville for most of his working life where he runs House of Gold music.

"MOONDREAMS"

With the Dick Jacobs Orchestra; recorded in stereo at Coral Record Studios, Pythian Temple, New York, 21st October 1958

Buddy was familiar with this Petty composition as he had played guitar on a 1957 session with the Norman Petty Trio when an instrumental version was cut. Holly handles the melancholy number well, in a performance fans tend to either dislike or to rate highly.

The number was written by Norman Petty and although not the producer on this last studio session he may have been present in New York and if so doubtless contributed some input. Ultimately the recording became a posthumous release as the flip of *"True Love Ways"* in 1960.

All four songs - from the October session - have seen release as both mono and stereo masters.

THE ARTHUR MURRAY DANCE PARTY

The Crickets performed live on this regular TV show back in December of '57, just after Niki Sullivan left the group and they became a trio.

The film clip of their performance is often screened (they sang *"Peggy Sue"*) and was used on a Dick Clark video release as his own footage of The Crickets film on Bandstand had been destroyed sometime in the '70s. The Arthur Murray show was transmitted in colour but only a black and white kinescope of the performance remains.

"MY TWO TIMIN' WOMAN"

Recorded at home on a wire recorder around 1949

Undoubtedly the first 'recording' of Buddy which dates from 1949 when he was 13 years of age. Not surprisingly his voice had not yet broken.

The song was written by country great Hank Snow and was pretty popular in the South around that time. Buddy's version was eventually released by brother Larry Holley, on his own label.

JERRY NAYLOR

A native of Texas , who was in the Crickets line-up during the early '60s, although he tends to give the impression that he was member of the original quartet, when Holly was the lead singer! Despite his memory having occasional lapses, he has, nevertheless done his best to promote the name of Buddy Holly via documentary-style programmes, down the years.

Naylor was the lead voice on a whole string of post-Holly Crickets Liberty recordings before being sidelined with heart problems at an early age. He has since worked in and around the music business , either as a performer or as a disc jockey, and in this latter category he hosted a particular fine Holly anniversary programme several years ago.

JACK NEAL

See entry - BUDDY AND JACK

Jerry, Buddy and Joe B. at City Hall, Newcastle, 6th March 1958.

RAY NEEDHAM

Co-founded the British Buddy Holly Society back in 1981 with Trevor Lailey and has always been in the forefront in promoting Holly's name in the UK.

As a senior police officer Ray has often used his investigative style to help unravel some of the little researched aspects of Buddy's career. We all owe him a debt.

RICKY NELSON

Sadly also a late, great, having lost his life in a Texas plan crash on New Year's Eve, 1985. The members of his backing band also perished in the tragedy and only the pilot and co-pilot of the re-conditioned DC-3 survived.

Evidently Buddy Holly and Ricky Nelson only met once although it is believe Nelson rated Holly very highly and usually featured *"Rave On"* in his stage act. On 30th December 1985 he played his final concert in Gunterville, Florida - evidently he performed *"Rave On"* as his last song to the full house audience. If so his final words would have been - 'Rave on for me'. Not a bad epitaph, eh?

Ricky Nelson left a long and varied recording output. Although stories indicate that he drifted into singing, he came from a highly musical background and was a professional musician through and through. A real modern day troubadour. Born 8th May 1940 he was aged 45 at the time of his untimely death.

Ricky's version of Holly's *"True Love Ways"* has since received a posthumous release.

NEW YORK

The T-shirts proclaim that Buddy Holly was a 'good ol' boy' and he was about as Texan as you can get, with his parents having also been born there. Remember that, although part of the Union, Texas is as near to a country as you can get being 267,300 square miles in area and 938 miles from the Northern border, to the Rio Grande on the edge of Mexico. That's big!

But after marrying in Lubbock in August '58, Buddy and Maria headed for New York and settled in an apartment in The Brevoort building on 8th Street, which is within the area commonly known as Greenwich Village. That was his base for the 6 months up to his death and whilst he retained business contacts in Texas he may well have shuttled between the two localities.

Certainly Buddy was no stranger to The Big Apple - the phrase had not been coined then by the way - having stopped off at venues there on most tours at least a dozen times. Several of his major TV appearances had also been in New York and of course, he had recorded studio sessions both at Bell Sound Studio in '57 and twice in the Pythian Temple during 1958. If we include the 'apartment tapes' material then Buddy recorded around 20 numbers overall in New York - one fifth of his total musical output.

The short New York period was to be most significant for Holly, both in musical and in personal terms.

TERRY NOLAND

Born Abilene, Texas and joined the Four Teens group in 1956, the personnel of which included a very youthful Joe B Mauldin, as well as Larry Welborn. Noland was a friend and contemporary of Buddy Holly but sadly no photo of the two together exists.

Noland recorded several solo sessions at Norman Petty's Clovis studios during 1957 and at one of these Trini Lopez (The Big Beats) played lead guitar. As can be seen from this book there were a lot of good musicians passing through Clovis.

Terry Noland and Buddy Holly kept in touch after Holly hit the big time and there is correspondence between the two dated late December 1958. In it Buddy suggests Noland consider using notable record producer Jessie Stone (see separate entry). This and other projects were left to wither on the vine when fate stepped in on that February night.

NOR VA JAK

Norman Petty used Nor-Va-Jak Records and Nor-Va-Jak Publishing as names for two of his business enterprises. The name was taken from the names of The Norman Petty Trio (Norman/Violet/Jack) to produce a highly distinctive identity.

These were both based at the Petty's 7th Street recording headquarters in Clovis, New Mexico. See entry Norman and Vi Petty.

'NOT FADE AWAY'

Film

This is the Buddy Holly film that never was . The basic story was written by Tom Drake and Jerry Allison and revolved around the events surrounding the Texan group being booked onto an all-black bill at the Apollo theatre. Shooting actually got underway sometime around 1975 before things were aborted. Of course, the later Holly film biog. included a classic sequence using the very same events.

"NOT FADE AWAY"

Recorded at Norman Petty Studios, Clovis, New Mexico, 29th May 1957. No bass on session but Jerry Allison cardboard box on percussion. Backing vocals, Buddy, Jerry and Niki Sullivan

Q: When is a 'B' side not a 'B' side?

A: When its *"Not Fade Away"*

An interesting recording that was first released tucked away on the flip of *"Oh Boy!"*. Although a Crickets recording it is only one of three tracks that doesn't feature a dubbed vocal backing by either The Picks or The Roses. This has Buddy, Jerry and Niki doing the honours - Niki's only involvement with the track. Also noteworthy is the percussion which is courtesy of Jerry beating upon a cardboard box.

The Holly/Petty composition is something of a steal of the Bo Diddley beat although it's not infringing any copyright. If Bo Diddley was upset he's never shown it and has dignified the situation by recording his own excellent version of *"Not Fade Away"*.

There is no doubt that the Holly/Crickets recording has grown in stature over the years and the phrase has almost entered the vocabulary. Perhaps the earliest impetus was The Rolling Stones decision to record the song in '64 - it was their first major hit. In the Holly film biography the number is the last song in the Clear Lake Medley - forming a dramatic climax to the film.

An undubbed first take of *"Not Fade Away"* by the Crickets has been released but differs little from the well known version.

"NOW WE'RE ONE"

Recorded at The Pythian Temple, Coral Records Studios, New York, 19th June 1958. Backed by Coral session musicians.

Recorded at the same New York session as *"Early In The Morning"*, it also shared the distinction of being a Bobby Darin composition. Both artists had July '58 releases of the same number - Holly as Coral single 9-62006 and Darin (styled as Rinky-dinks) on Atco 6121. They were each US hits, but only entered the lower region of the charts.

"Now We're One" was included on Volume 2 of the Buddy Holly Story album back in 1960 but has appeared on little else since. Played at Holly's own Texas wedding in August '58 it should surely have been included in the 'Love Songs' album several years back, but was presumably overlooked. While the cling-cling piano and the girlie backing group give the record a dated sound, Holly's vocal is accomplished and as ever, highly distinctive.

JOHNNY O'KEEFE

One of a very small group of '50s Australian rock'n'roll artists who was virtually unknown in both the UK and the USA.

Although not listed on most posters he opened the Crickets Australian tour shows (see separate entry) and presumably included his domestic hit recording *"Wild One"*. It is this song that Jerry Allison took a liking to and cut as IVAN with the amended title *"Real Wild Child"*. (A few years earlier a controversial Brando film 'The Wild One' had been partly banned and to re-title the disc was no doubt an obvious prudent step).

O'Keefe died prematurely several years ago whilst still in his 40s.

'OFF THE RECORD'

A typically staid '50s TV show in this country which was hosted by former big band artist Jack Payne. Before the 2nd World War Payne had hosted the BBC Dance Orchestra which, at one time, had Jack Jackson - that grand-daddy of DJs - also in its ranks. The fact that Jack Payne had been in the record business since the '20s surely made him a doubtful choice to host a topical music programme. However, in '58 youth culture was not yet all pervasive.

'Off The Record' was one of the few television vehicles for visiting US rock artists and one suspected Jack Payne tolerated the music, even if he seldom waxed enthusiastic. The Crickets performance was telerecorded and there has been ongoing doubt as to whether they mimed their number (*"Maybe Baby"*) or performed, in effect, 'live'. The question has been settled this very year (1994) with a audio recording having come to light finally confirming that Holly sang live vocals on the programme.

Hopefully, the tape - when cleaned up - will eventually get released in some way, if it can be legally arranged.

Buddy Holly — in smilingly pensive mood. March '58 during UK tour.

"OH BOY!"

Recorded at Norman Petty's Clovis, New Mexico Studios, between 29th Jun/1st Jul '57. The Crickets were a trio on this recording. The Picks overdubbed backing vocals, added later.

Intriguing to think that when the group recorded this number, *"That'll Be The Day"* was still 'in the can' and a release date had not been scheduled. *"Oh Boy!"* was to become a monster hit for the quartet although rhythm guitarist Niki Sullivan didn't actually play on the session. Also recorded on the same day were *"Listen To Me"* and *"Peggy Sue"* - three classic numbers.

Even today the recording of *"Oh Boy!"* comes over as a high energy performance that is difficult to better. Sonny West and Bill Tilghman were the main writers on both this and *"Rave On"* with Norman adding his name, although one senses the songs were basically written before being brought to Clovis.

"Oh Boy!" was a major hit on both sides of the Atlantic and with *"Peggy Sue"* still on the charts Holly was established as anything but a one-hit wonder. A label to be avoided at all costs, both then and now.

In the last few years an unauthorised release of *"Oh Boy!"* by The Crickets, with The Picks backing vocals being omitted, has cropped up. It is to be hoped that an official release will follow at some point. Similarly The Crickets televised '58 appearance has come out on record but not an official release via MCA. (The three tracks performed; *"That'll Be The Day"*, *"Peggy Sue"* and *"Oh Boy!"* are poorly recorded and of interest only from a nostalgic viewpoint).

An earlier live performance from the Ed Sullivan Show where The Crickets performed *"Oh Boy!"* as a trio is available via a videogram and the sound is much better.

"Oh Boy!" has been heavily covered over the years with Mud taking it to No.1 in 1975 with their own distinctive interpretation.

THE LONDON PALLADIUM, ENGLAND

Buddy Holly and The Crickets achieved the accolade of playing the Palladium when they were over here on their only UK tour. On Sunday, 2nd March 1958 they closed the first half of the televised show, the headliner that day being another American, Bob Hope, who they met briefly and that same day they also fitted in two shows at Kilburn which meant a quick dash around the postal districts of London was presumably the order of the day.

Memories of their first national TV appearance are mixed. They rushed through three numbers in just over six minutes and the aural evidence that survives on bootleg albums is less than impressive. But the London Palladum was *the* venue and undoubtedly one of the most prestigious shows of their career.

35 years later and The Crickets have played the Palladium once again.

ROY ORBISON

Died 6th December 1988: aged 52

Roy Kelton Orbison was born on 23rd April 1936 with both the towns of Vernon and Wink in Texas claiming him as their native son after fame struck.

Although with the passage of time we tend to think of Orbison and Holly as direct contemporaries Roy had only regional success in the early years and he did not blitz the charts until almost 18 months after Holly had died. Their paths had seldom crossed although Orbison did briefly record as the Teen Kings in Clovis before making his way to Memphis and Sun Records. Certainly two Orbison compositions (*"An Empty Cup"* and *"You've Got Love"*) got passed onto The Crickets via Norman Petty and made their way on to 'The Chirping Crickets' album. In an interview Roy Orbison spoke fondly of spending a day in Holly's company and forming a fast friendship.

Had Holly lived , one wonders if there would have been room for two heavy-spectacled Texan singers in the business. Certainly their images do overlap somewhat.

Little else links the two, although Orbison's first wife, Claudette used to attend Lubbock High School in the '50s

THE BROOKLYN PARAMOUNT, NEW YORK

Probably equivalent to the London Palladium, the Paramount theatre was the mecca for American rock'n'roll performers during the '50s. The aura of these times was lovingly recreated on screen in '78 when Alan Freed's film biography 'American Hot Wax' was released (by Paramount Pictures no less).

The Crickets actually appeared at The Paramount in both 1957 and 1958 as part of major rock'n'roll package shows that criss-crossed the country. The superb colour shot which adorns the cover of 'The Chirping Crickets' album was actually taken on the roof of that same theatre during their first appearance there. (Likewise the photo that adorns the cover of this book).

If anyone points out that there were two Paramount Theatre (Brooklyn and New York) you could just be right!

COLONEL TOM PARKER

This legendary individual - an honorary colonel only - was manager of the late, great Elvis Presley from 15th March 1956 up until his client's premature death in August 1977. Born Andreas Cornelius Van Kujik in Holland, 1909 he continuously wielded a tight grip over Presley's affairs that was only relinguished after court-room litigation ruled against him following Elvis' demise.

There is speculation that at some time in '55, Col. Parker was sounded out concerning managing the career of the embryonic Holly - still Buddy Holley at that time. This would seem improbable, but not impossible, although to imagine such a pairing is too bizarre. 'Buddy and the Colonel' just doesn't have the same ring to it!

SUE PARRISH

Local Lubbock song-writer who collaborated with Holly in the early years by penning two of the numbers that he recorded in Nashville on his first visit there in January 1956.

Buddy hardly knew of her before she wrote to him offering him some songs she had written. Sue Parrish eventually moved away from Lubbock and settled in the California area.

GORDON PAYNE

From Oklahoma, USA Gordon Payne is the present lead singer with The Crickets and whilst not a household name he has held that position for longer than Holly himself ever did. Whilst Joe B Mauldin and Jerry Allison remain with the group the personnel has seen numerous changes over the years but with Jerry very much the common denominator.

Gordon plays powerful lead guitar, a stratocaster of course and manages to avoid plagiarising Holly's style. He was for years a member of Waylon Jennings back-up band and earlier still had cut solo records without notable success.

Apart from performing lead vocals and playing guitar he has also co-written much of The Crickets current material including the track which accurately describes them; *"Three piece"*.

BOBBY PEEPLES

An obscure name except to the most fanatical Holly followers. Bobby Peeples was a school friend of Holly at Lubbock High School and had access to an acetate disc-cutter in the early '50s and this was a godsend to Holly/Montgomery who were anxious to make demos in their quest to get a break.

All the undubbed garage-type material on the 1986 'Something Special' Roller-coaster album was recorded by Peeples who became lost to sight at some undetermined point. It was thought he may have recorded a live Carlsbad, New Mexico concert and his whereabouts became increasingly frustrating for fans. He was located, in Texas, a few years ago by English super-fan Ray Needham and this confirmed that no 'live' footage was laying around waiting to be unearthed.

PEGGY SUE GARRON

Former wife of J I Allison, drummer and co-founder of The Crickets. They married in '58 and jointly went on honeymoon with Buddy and Maria to Acapulco, Mexico.

She remains famous for inadvertantly giving her name to one of the most seminal of all rock'n'roll anthems, *"Peggy Sue"*. However she has no connection with the music industry and these days runs a plumbing business.

Peggy Sue recently visited the UK to promote the showing of a short TV feature, which told of her part in the Buddy Holly legend. In an amazing coincidence it was found that she and Donna Ludwig, the ex-beau of Ritchie Valens, were actually living close to one another in the same town. Remembering that Ritchie and Donna came from California it really seems one big coincidence.

Peggy Sue and Jerry divorced after nine years of marriage. See also entries under JERRY ALLISON AND IVAN.

"PEGGY SUE"

Recorded at Norman Petty studios, between 29th June and 1st July 1957. Group - Buddy/Jerry/Joe. See below re. Niki Sullivan

This most famous of compositions was attributed to Buddy, Jerry and manager, Norman Petty. Recorded in pretty quick order it started out as *"Cindy Lou"* but ended up instead having the name of Jerry's girlfriend as the title. The story goes that when practised in its original state it had more of a calypso rhythm.

"Peggy Sue" became Holly's first solo hit and was high in the Top 10 on both sides of the Atlantic. At the time the track was laid down, The Crickets were a quartet but all Niki Sullivan got to do was to flick the treble switch on Buddy's fender to facilitate that great guitar solo. The recording the world is familiar with is Take 2 but the first take has been released on a European album and differs little. Probably Holly's vocal mannerisms includes less 'hiccups'. The Picks have also overdubbed Holly's vocal on a recent re-issue and whilst this style works well on some of the Nashville tracks, it is less successful on classics such as *"Peggy Sue"* and *"Everyday"*.

Three separate live versions of *"Peggy Sue"* are in circulation.In chronological order these are the first Ed Sullivan show, the Aurthur Murray Show and from the UK the performance at the London Palladium. Finally, Holly recorded a 24 second radio jingle (to the tune of *"Peggy Sue"*) and this is worth seeking out.

"PEGGY SUE GOT MARRIED"

Taped at Holly's New York flat, 5th December 1958

One of six tracks recorded at the home on Buddy's Ampex tape recorder in the run-up to Christmas, 1958. All are self-compositions but this one is a cleverly constructed sequel to *"Peggy Sue"*. Evidently Buddy's father had suggested the basic idea for the song.

Heavily overdubbed by Coral's Jack Hansen within months of Holly's death, the single made the Top 20 in the UK but did little in the US. Later both the undubbed version and a second dubbed version masterminded by Norman Petty and very similar instrumentally to *"Peggy Sue"*, were released and formed part of the MCA box-set.

As with *"Crying, Waiting, Hoping"* a stereo master was not made and the Hansen dubbed performance is available in mono only.

The song itself has seldom been covered although Mike Berry used it (as Kenny Lord and the Statesmen) when cutting a 1959 demo record for submitting to Joe Meek. If it has been neglected it got a real shot in the arm a few years ago when it was used as the title and theme tune for the much acclaimed film, starring Kathleen Turner, which was set in or around 1962.

CARL PERKINS

Born on 9th April 1932, in Lake City Tennessee, Carl is one of the all-time greats of the '50s rock'n'roll principally through having written and recorded *"Blue Suede Shoes"*. In fact that was his one and only major hit record: it's really hard to realise that he hasn't had a whole string of them such is his fame.

Apart from *"Blue Suede Shoes"* Carl has written a series of rock'n'roll standards and three of them were recorded by The Beatles - which doubtless swelled Carl's bank account. (Bought his parents a farm or so the story goes).

Carl's greatest recordings were on Sun although he also cut a lot of fine sides for Columbia. Holly and Carl only met once or twice and the Tennessean has spoken movingly - in interviews - of their immediate warm empathy.

PETER AND GORDON

A UK vocal duo who had a string of British hits in the '60s before going their separate ways. Gordon Waller into eventual obscurity whilst Peter Asher - who almost became Beatle Paul's brother-in-law - stayed in the music business over the years with significant success.

Their version of *"True Love Ways"* gave the song its greatest ever chart success but it is surely one of the least appealing versions of the song.

But one always felt that Asher had an affinity with Holly's music and it is not surprising that he produced a whole series of Holly-associated songs for Linda Ronstadt, two of which (*"That'll Be The Day"* and *"It's So Easy"*) were major chart records for her in the '70s.

ROGER PETERSON

Roger Arthur Peterson was the 21 year old pilot of the Beechcraft Bonanza aircraft which crashed five miles north-west of Mason City one day in the early hours of February 1959, sadly killing all four of the plane's occupants.

Remembering that the loss must have been as great for Peterson's family, it was gratifying to learn that his name was included on the permanent memorial to the singers that was erected a few years ago at The Surf Ballroom, Clear Lake, Iowa.

See also CIVIL AERONAUTICS BOARD REPORT

NORMAN AND VI PETTY

Norman Petty set-up a recording studio in Clovis, New Mexico in 1950, the year after he had formed The Norman Petty Trio which comprised of his wife Vi Petty, Jack Vaughn and Norman himself. Buddy Holly gravitated to the studios in late '56 and eventually recorded that most famous of all demos, *"That'll Be The Day"* in Clovis late February 1957. The studios later acquired the name of NorVaJack being an amalgam of the trio member names - see separate entry NOR VA JACK.

One of the first independent record producers of the rock'n'roll era, Norman also became the manager of The Crickets and produced those famous '57/58 sessions that , in retrospect, has to be Buddy's most fertile recording period. Petty's name is shown as part - composer on many of the most famous Holly numbers despite the fact that he himself didn't read music. However he was exceptionally musical and doubtless contributed something to various compositions - but just how much will always remain problematical. Both Norman (piano/organ) and Vi (piano) occasionally played on Holly recording sessions.

Norman Petty had the most wonderful speaking voice and do seek out, if you can some of the interview material he has been involved with. The Norman Petty story is a long and involved one and produced major hits with a variety of artists over the years. Probably the best known of those being The Stringalongs and The Fireballs.

Tragically Norman Petty succumbed to leukemia in 1984, having been hospitalised in Lubbock Methodist Hospital. Coincidently Jack Vaughn, guitarist with the Trio died the same year while the last member of the group, Vi Petty, died as recently as 1992.

Violet Petty was always known affectionately to Buddy and the boys by the nickname Pansy.

CHARLIE PHILLIPS

Little known country artist born close to the Texas/New Mexico border in Farwell, Texas. He wrote and recorded the popular number *"Sugartime"* back in '57 and the McGuire Sisters had a US No. 1 record with it the following January.

At the time Charlie recorded his version in Petty's Clovis studio Buddy was ever-present and it was natural for him to play lead guitar on the session. Jack Vaughn of The Norman Petty Trio also helped out instrumentally on the track.

Apart from playing lead on the flip, *"One Faded Rose"*, Buddy also performed harmony vocals. Both tracks are virtually impossible to find in their original 45 rpm state.

SAM PHILLIPS

Born 1923,Alabaman Sam Phillips formed the Memphis Phillip's International label in 1950 and its more famous associate, Sun records, just two years later. In the early explosion of rock'n'roll dozens of Southern artists gravitated to the door of his Union Avenue studio to try and persuade Sam to record them, with varying degrees of success. Was Buddy one of them? See SUN RECORDS entry and below.

Elvis, Jerry Lee and Johnny Cash were three of the names that did achieve fame in a big way, but others such as Roy Orbison achieved little but regional success via Sam. Still other notables, such as Johnny Burnette and his Trio, were rejected at the outset. Rumours did arise that Buddy may have tried the Sun route but with superb facilites on his doorstep in Clovis it is debatable. (Roy Orbison tried both avenues - recording first for Norman Petty before linking up with Sam Phillips).

Phillips has attained his own special niche in rock'n'roll by nurturing his great discovery, Elvis, before pointing him on the way to everlasting stardom with RCA.Sam's brother, Judd Phillips,who did so much to help Sam distribute his records in the early days has passed away this year (1994) .

THE PICKS

The group comprised brothers Bill and John Pickering and friend Bob Lapham. They were responsible for the vocal backings on most of The Crickets famous '57 recordings before being replaced by The Roses the following year. Sadly Bill Pickering died back in 1985, at age 57, just the year after they had completed a major project to dub backing vocals onto a whole host of Holly recordings in an attempt to give them a more distinctive 'Chirping Crickets' sound.

The posthumous overdubs were done with great love and affection but they have met with a very mixed response from long-time fans. Having been familiar with recordings over a period of nearly 30 years it is exceptionally difficult for fans to judge such 'amended' recordings dispassionately. Interestingly, whilst the over-dubs were submitted to MCA in the '80s they were eventually released on The Picks own record label, Pick Records.

The trio think that maybe they were the best vocal group of '57, rather than Jerry, Joe B and Niki, who were largely instrumentalists only at that time. Rather academic really but no one can grudge The Picks their efforts to achieve belated recognition for the part they played in Holly's recording career.

ELVIS PRESLEY

Buddy Holly and Elvis first met as Presley frequently toured the Southern states in '54/'55 and Lubbock, Texas was often part of the itinerary. Holly is said to have picked up Elvis in his car and showed Elvis the sights - such as they were! There is a 1955 photo of Elvis (probably taken at The Cotton Club) with Buddy and Bob Montgomery in close proximity. Buddy, Bob and Larry Welborn performed as opening spot on one of Elvis' earliest Lubbock concerts and there is no doubt that Holly was heavily influenced by Elvis in the composition of his backing group and in material. Interestingly Presley's first dates described him as 'The King of Western Bop' - Buddy's visiting card stated 'Western and Bop'.

The bootleg-style Atlas album 'Elvis and Buddy' alternates seven songs which both artists recorded, and makes for interesting comparisons. However , the Elvis recordings were all studio performances, whilst those by Holly are largely demo-type efforts. Elsewhere, there is one recording to be avoided at all costs - an apparent 'duet' by Elvis and Buddy of *"Ready Teddy"*. It is nothing more than the two records played simultaneously. Unfortunately they were recorded at different tempos!

Although Presley and Holly never met after 1955, there was a bond. Elvis sent a telegram to Buddy's parents from Germany at the time of his death and in later years he was quoted as saying that Buddy was his favourite rock & roll singer. Both are legends.

Elvis was born in Tupelo, Mississippi, 8th January 1935 and died prematurely on 16th August 1977 in Memphis Tennessee.

PRISM RECORDS

The record label that never was - officially. This was one of several projects that was in embryo at the time of Holly's death. Maria Music, for publishing, was another.

Buddy Holly would have been President of Prism, which would have been based in Clovis, New Mexico. Ray Rush (one of The Roses) was slotted in as Promotions Manager while Norman Petty was listed as Sales. This format was mooted prior to Buddy's split with Norman, so what would have been the final format of Prism Records we will never know.

In the last year or two 'The Apartment Tapes' have been issued on a bootleg-style album which has the label/number; Prism Records - 819. So a very different Prism label has come into existence - via the back door.

"QUEEN OF THE BALLROOM"

Buddy and Bob performance at radio station KDAV. Circa '54/'55

Believed written by Lubbock bassist Don Guess, this was one of the compositions that was eventually issued posthumously under the Buddy and Bob banner. In the UK this came out in 1965 on the 'Holly In The Hills' album, although it was omitted from the US album of the same name.

A fairly routine country-ish number, the mono release of this item has some instrumental overdubbing. It has not been released in its original format and is unlikely to be put out commercially.

"RAINING IN MY HEART"

With the Dick Jacobs Orchestra.Recorded in stereo at Coral Record Studios, Pythian Temple, New York, 21st October 1958

One of Holly's greatest ever solo recordings that continues to get airplay to the present day despite not achieving hit status. Instead it was the flip of *"It Doesn't Matter Anymore"*, which became a major posthumous hit on both sides of the Atlantic in 1959. *"Raining In My Heart"* was written by the legendary songwriting duo of Boudleaux and Felice Bryant and was presumably passed to Buddy via his friend Phil Everly for what was to be Holly's final studio recording session.

Although recorded in stereo, the single was a mono master and for a great many years the track was not readily available in its stereo format except in the US where it had appeared on a compilation LP. (It was not until 1986 that a commemorative UK release in stereo came about).

Holly's version has often been plagiarised in TV adverts and the phrase now seems to have entered the public's general consciousness. Has not, surprisingly, been much covered, although Leo Sayer had a minor hit with it in the '70s.

Buddy's brother Larry always quotes this number as his favourite by Buddy and it's easy to understand why.

The song is not to be confused with the 'R&B' hit by the late Slim Harpo which has the same title.

BOOTS RANDOLPH (AND SAXOPHONES)

By virtue of the Crickets line-up Buddy Holly rarely came into contact with that most inspired of musical instruments, the saxophone, but when he did the results were memorable.

The last of Holly's Decca sessions in Nashville (November '56) is believed to feature Boots Randolph on what would have been one of hundreds of sessions for producer Owen Bradley, prior to Boots own solo success on *"Yakety Sax"*. Of the three tracks recorded both 'Ollie Vee and *"Modern Don Juan"* have creditable sax work. It also seems to be lurking in the background of the ballad, *"You Are My One Desire"*, the last of the numbers attempted.

Buddy next used a saxophone at his mid-'58 session in New York when he cut *"Early In The Morning"* at short notice using much the same set-up as Bobby Darin used for his version. The marvellous searing sax is courtesy of Sam 'The Man' Taylor - whose pedigree included working with Louis Jordan - and who himself released a string of instrumental albums on US Decca over the years.

Within three months Buddy had recruited the legendary saxophonist King Curtis to perform a one-off Clovis session which produced both Waylon Jennings first single as well as two tracks of Holly himself, although they were not to be released in his lifetime.

Finally, at Buddy's last Coral recording session, Boomie Richman played a mellow tenor sax which only comes through as a solo on one of the four tracks, *"True Love Ways"*. It is hard to imagine the solo being bettered and invariably other versions have reproduced his solo, note for note.

As Buddy Holly continually experimented musically he would doubtless have tried further work with this most famous of reed instruments.

"RAVE ON"

Recorded at Bell Sound, Studios, New York on 25th January 1958. Jerry and Joe B on backing instrumentals together with Al Caiola (guitar) and Norman Petty (piano). Background vocals - session singers.

This is the '50s track that has the dubious honour of being described as 'music to steal hub-caps by'. Surely one of the silliest quotes to emanate from a paranoid older generation that felt threatened by the unfamiliar music they were hearing for the first time. The phrase 'Rave on' was first heard as part of the lyrics in the 1956 Carl Perkins number *"Dixie Fried"*, which is doubtless how Bill Tilghman and Sonny West got the idea for their song.

"Rave On" is an absolute gem and the West/Tilghman partnership had also been responsible for the hit *"Oh Boy!"* just a few months earlier. Buddy and the boys have travelled up to New York for TV dates after Christmas, 1957 and managed to fit in the session at the end of a tour which had been headlined by The Everly Brothers.

The song was a Top 5 hit in both the US and the UK and has to be one of Holly's best remembered recordings. Whilst there have been several laudable versions of *"Rave On"* over the years, none has the impact which Holly's stretched opening syllable gives his recording.

Sadly, the first two takes of *"Rave On"* have never been recovered, although they were supposedly returned to Norman Petty in Clovis.

"READY TEDDY"

Recorded at Norman Petty Studios, Clovis, New Mexico between May/July 1957. Solo release. Crickets a quartet - plus Vi Petty (piano)

"Ready Teddy" was written by John Marascalco and Bumps Blackwell and had been a No. 1 record for Little Richard in 1956 on the R&B charts. Elvis recorded his version later in '56 and frequently featured it, as did Buddy, in live performances.

Holly's version was recorded with his first solo album in mind but he made few concessions in cutting the number and it is anything but a filler in an all-out vocal performance that matches Little Richard in its power. The instrumentation is also first rate in what is a very tight group sound.

Latterly, a grotesque 'duet' of *"Ready Teddy"* between Elvis and Buddy was released on a foreign album but it is not recommended unless you have masochist tendencies.

RECORD LABELS

Buddy Holly's first recording contract was as a solo artist for the US Decca label and his complete output for them was recorded over three sessions in Nashville during 1956. Producer on each occasion was Owen Bradley - see separate entry.

With his career going nowhere Buddy - now part of the Crickets - signed with Brunswick and their subsequent recordings were released on that Decca subsidiary. Meanwhile Petty arranged for solo recordings by Holly - usually featuring the same personnel - to be released through Decca's more prestigious label, Coral. This is the label that Buddy was contracted to at the time of his death while the Crickets, with replacement lead singer Earl Sinks, had recorded a new single in November 1958 that was released on Coral Records both here and in the States.

(In the UK Holly/Crickets recordings during 1957/8 were all released on Coral with Brunswick being the vehicle for the Nashville recordings only).

Holly product has over the years been leased by his recording company (now styled MCA) to a whole collection of labels.

Bootleg-style releases have also proliferated in recent years with MCA reluctant or unable to put out little apart from re-issues of Greatest Hits - type collections.

The continuing absence of a definitive box-set collection of all Holly/Crickets recordings on compact disc remains a major oversight bearing in mind the wealth of additional material that has surfaced over the last 15 years. CDs themselves have been about since 1982 and there are still Holly recordings not available in that format.

In the '60s an article in the musical press discussed Holly releases under the heading 'The Long Waiting Game'. Despite the appearance of a vinyl/cassette box set in 1979 the situation remains frustrating and disappointing to the hard-core Holly fans. The waiting game continues.

"REMINISCING"

Session at Norman Petty Studios, Cliovis, New Mexico inc. King Curtis on sax - 10th September 1958

The backround to this recording is fully described under the heading of King Curtis elsewhere in this book.

A posthumous single release for Holly in 1962 "*Reminiscing*" acted as a trailer for the album of the same name which belatedly hit the shops the following year. Both the single and the album had chart success in the UK but made little impact in the US itself.

Despite being listed as a King Curtis composition it was learnt recently that it was written by Holly himself. In retrospect this makes sense as whilst Curtis Ousley was a talented musician, and composed scores of instrumental numbers, he wasn't noted for his lyrics! Over the years the song has attracted few covers although a Beatles version from their Hamburg days has been released. A second-wave San Francisco group, the Flamin' Groovies, also recorded the song in the '70s.

The Holly version we are familiar with includes dubbed instrumentation via The Fireballs. The undubbed version has only been released to date as bootleg material.

For completists the original UK 45 release has a guitar line omitted - it having been added for the album release only

LITTLE RICHARD

Born 25th December 1932

It is quite certain that Buddy Holly was a big fan of Richard Wayne Penniman and the two met back in Lubbock well before Holly hit the big-time. For a solid 2½ years from late '55 until 1958 Richard was a virtual ever-present in the US charts and when he gave up rock'n'roll (and found God) the event was listed as a watershed in the music.

It is sometimes hard today to remember just how influential Richard was on his fellow performers.Elvis led the pack with three Penniman hits (*"Rip It Up"* / *"Ready Teddy"* / *"Long Tall Sally"*) on his second album release and others followed. While artists such as Holly and Vincent recorded powerful versions of Richard material, Pat Boone went for sanitised covers so as to appeal to the masses. Strangely the biggest influence that Richard had on Buddy was on the latter's guitar style which often incorporated Little Richard's straight-8 rhythm.

While Buddy Holly never commerically recorded a Penniman composition (*"Slippin' And Slidin'"* was a practice tape) he certainly performed his material routinely on stage with *"Keep A Knockin'"* and *"Tutti Frutti"* being especial favourites. Holly's own recording of *"Well . . . All right"* was inspired by Richard's frequent exclamation of these three words.

It is disappointing that the linked memory of Holly/Richard has been tarnished by dubious quotes from the veteran singer about Holly that cannot be readily challenged 30 years on.

"RIP IT UP"

Practice tape; recorded in Lubbock late '56/early '57

Composed by erstwhile Little Richard chauffeur, John Marascalco and Speciality producer, Bumps Blackwell, *"Rip It Up"* was a hit for both Richard and Bill Haley in '56 and would have been standard bandstand material for most rock'n'rollers of the age.

Certainly Holly was no exception and his rehearsal-type version, also from 1956, was not a studio performance as such. *"Rip It Up"* together with a mixed bag of material was released in 1964 as part of the 'Showcase' album, albeit heavily overdubbed instrumentally. The untouched mono recording wasn't released until two decades later.

MARTY ROBBINS

Charismatic country artist who died prematurely in 1982 at the early age of 57, just shortly after appearing in Clint Eastwood's film 'Honky Tonk Man' and in which he performed the title track.

It is well known that Marty Robbin's manager Eddie Crandall helped in getting Buddy the chance to cut demo records which were subsequently sent on to Nashville and led to his first recording contract.

Certainly Marty Robbins recorded very much in the rockabilly vein himself back in '55/'56 even covering the Elvis release of *"That's All Right"*. He later became a country superstar but was always ready to reminisce and discuss the early days when Buddy, Jerry and Joe hung around his office. He had fond memories of Buddy who he remembered as being completely besotted with the music, style and appearance of Elvis Presley.

The paths of Marty Robbins and Holly rarely crossed after those early days but both are major artists who contributed much to the music scene which they both left much too early.

Marty was born on 26th September 1925 and died 8th December 1982.

JIM ROBINSON

Texan singer who never achieved national success but at least two of his recordings (*"Whole Lotta Lovin'"* /*"It's A Wonderful Feeling"*) feature Holly on lead guitar, having been cut at Norman Petty's studios in early '57. On a couple of the tracks, Jerry Allison uses a cardboard box instead of his drum-kit, a forerunner to the session where they cut *"You're So Square"* and Jerry used the same technique

Many of the tracks on which Holly backed other artists - he was virtually a session guitarist at Clovis in the first half of '57 -are available on a European album entitled 'Artistry On Guitar Signed Buddy Holly': NorVaJak 816. Look for it through specialist outlets.

RED ROBINSON

Unknown on these shores, Red Robinson was Canada's premier DJ back when rock'n'roll ruled the airwaves. He did a lengthy interview with Holly backstage at the Georgia Auditorium, Vancouver, 23rd October 1957 at a time when interviews with rock artists tended to be both banal and brief. His interview - which we first heard in 1980 - is lengthy and less superficial than, for example the Dick Clark Bandstand interview. It was to be several years before rock stars were interviewed in greater depth and the music started to be dissected and analysed almost adnauseum.

Photos of Red Robinson from that era reveal a Jerry Lee Lewis clone while in the photo with Holly the singer has not yet acquired his solid-framed specs and his teeth have yet to be capped. In a Buddy Holly lookalike contest Holly would probably have tied for third place using this picture.

If and when a definitive CD box set is released it is to be hoped that this interview would be included.

"ROCK-A-BYE ROCK"

Demo recorded at Norman Petty Studios, Clovis, New Mexico,; Feb - Apr '56

A perfect example of the Buddy Holly knack of singing a patently rock'n'roll number while at the same time endowing the lyrics with a most plaintive vocal delivery.

A self-composition it was one of a batch of demo-style recordings that didn't see the light of day until the '60s, when a series of albums came out ('Reminiscing',' Showcase', etc.).

Again the released recording was heavily overdubbed a la Fireballs to produce a commercial, stereo release. It was later released (mono/undubbed) on the '86 LP 'For The First time Anywhere'.

The Holly recording with dubbed backing vocals by The Picks has also been released.

"ROCK AROUND WITH OLLIE VEE"

Versions recorded at second and third Nashville recording sessions, Bradley's Barn, 22nd July and 15th November 1956 respectively

Sonny Curtis wrote this most catchy of numbers and has featured it in his own stage act, through to the present day. He was present playing lead guitar on Holly's July recording but not on the later version when the song was transformed into a sax-based number. This sax cut of 'Ollie Vee was released as a Decca single in the US during September '57, probably as a direct result of *"That'll Be The Day"* going to No. 1. If record buyers bought it - and few did - they were in for a shock; the single's 'B' side was the much earlier recording of *"That'll Be The Day"* and vastly different to the slick, commercial hit waxing.

The alternate, saxophone version of 'Ollie Vee remained unissued in this country until '75 when all the Nashville material was released on one album, 'The Nashville Sessions'. Whilst the number has never been a hit it has always remained a favourite to jive to and has featured prominently in both the stage show and the film biography of Holly.

The Picks did vocal overdubs in 1984 of the 'guitar' version of the number. Ollie Vee, by the way, is the unusual name of a local person that Sonny knew back in Meadow, Texas.

"ROCK ME MY BABY"

Crickets recording cut on the road, Oklahoma City; Sept '57

One of the greatest examples of The Crickets work as a quartet. It was recorded with three other numbers at the Tinker Air Force Base, Oklahoma City, whilst the group were taking an enforced break from touring because of segregation problems. The whole thing is a gem, from the vocal itself to the ringing lead guitar solo to the perfect backing vocals of The Picks.

Written by songwriters Shorty Long and Susan Heather the recording formed part of 'The Chirping Crickets' album which was released here in March '58. Unfortunately separately published album charts didn't arise until The Melody Maker printed a Top 10 in November '58 so the album - statistically - was not a hit. But it was in every other respect and has often been included in all-time top 100 albums lists down the years.

TOMMY ROE

Born Thomas David Roe on 9th May 1942, Atlanta, Georgia, Tommy Roe had a whole cluster of hits in the US during a term that lasted some 10 years. Not only did his vocals lean somewhat on Holly's style but he virtually took over the *"Peggy Sue"* rhythm - especially with his first No. 1, *"Sheila"* in 1962 and several years later with *"Dizzy"*.

He has never been afraid to acknowledge his debt to Holly and during his stage act often includes a medley of Holly's hits. Strangely he has not recorded a full-blown tribute album but has recorded the occasional track (*"It Doesn't Matter Anymore"* / *"Raining In My Heart"*) at random times.

WESLEY ROSE

Born 1912

Son of Fred Rose, a founder of the giant Acuff Rose Music Publishing co., Wesley produced many major country artists for the likes of RCA, Mercury and other labels. He also formed the Hickory label and signed artists such as Roy Acuff, Don Gibson and the Kershaws.

His main involvement with the pop scene was to help launch the career of the Everly Brothers via Archie Bleyer's Cadence label. It is probable that Wesley Rose was instrumental in rejecting the two Holly demos that had been cut with The Everly Brothers in mind - one of those elusive facts it is impossible to confirm. Certainly the special friendship of the Crickets/Everly's was not affected and it remains to the present day.

Wesley Rose died in 1990.

THE ROSES

The Roses were used as the backing vocal group on later Crickets recordings replacing The Picks who had been used from early '57 through to the end of that year. The group consisted of Bob Linville, Ray Rush and David Bigham and their involvement differed significantly from The Picks in one respect - they actually toured with The Crickets on one unique occasion in '58. (Despite this fact Norman Petty still preferred to overdub backing vocals on Crickets material without the backing singers being present on the session. Consequently whilst Holly had met all the various backing vocalists they didn't exactly hang out together).

Later Ray Rush acted as A&R man on several David Box recordings and it seems had been lined up during late '58 to act as Promotions manager with Holly's embryonic Prism record label.

ROYAL TEENS

Little remembered group from the '50s that had just one big record "*Short Shorts*" a disc that in the trade, would have been called a novelty number. Their other claim to fame was that Bob Gaudio was briefly a member before joining The Four Seasons.

In 1958 lead singer Joey Villa was instrumental in introducing Lou Giordano to Buddy and Giordano became the protégé of Holly and Phil Everly , who co-produced his Brunswick single "*Stay Close to Me*". See LOU GIORDANO.

RUMOURS

Over a period of 35 years all sorts of rumours have come and gone concerning undiscovered Holly performances and most are hardly worth repeating, but a random sample are given below.

In the early days it was rumoured that a song title existed called *"So Rare"* which was a '57 instrumental hit for Jimmy Dorsey, but was unconnected in any way with Holly. For even longer the title *"I Tried To Forget"* was said to exist until it was realised it was just an alternate title for *"I Guess I Was Just A Fool"*.

In the '60s fans learnt through the musical press that the unknown 'Rutland Records' intended to put out a whole collection of unreleased material. It never happened. That was similar to the more recent publicity surrounding a US Live Gold release which eventually turned out to be virtually a re-release of tribute-type material, previously available as an import via Silhouette records. It certainly contained nothing devastatingly original.

A Dutch compilation album 'His Kind Of Music' has three tracks attributed to Buddy Holly and Larry Welborn but minimal research shows that these are '60s recordings. (Even easier is to just spin the recording and listen!).

Remembering back to the days of '59/'60 it was even rumoured that Holly hadn't perished after all, but was just badly mutilated! Contrarily - as more and more posthumous material came to light - it was suggested that all Holly releases might not be 100% authentic. Hard to imagine such thinking with the vantage point of hindsight.

Coming up to date we do know that there are odds and ends of Holly material which could still come out - see MAYBE BABY entry, etc. - but all studio masters have long since been released. Unless a piece of tape still exists somewhere amongst all the reels of recording paraphernalia in Clovis.

How's that for another rumour?

TOMMY SANDS

Little remembered Capitol recording artist from the '50s, whose other claim to fame is that he was, briefly, the son-in-law of singing legend, Frank Sinatra. It came to light a few years back that Graham Turnbull (aka Sonny Turner) had 'discovered' several songs that he had collaborated on with Buddy Holly, which had laid undisturbed for years in his guitar case.

Amongst these songs was one that was to be offered to Tommy Sands. In a bizarre twist to this story the late actor Audie Murphy - himself to be the victim of a 'plane crash - was name as a co-writer.

The whole thing is intriguing and perhaps further research could be done to find out whether (for example) Audie Murphy had any other connections with the music scene.

Buddy Holly in practice stance, UK Tour, March '58.

FRANKIE SARDO

Obscure singer from New York, of Italian extraction, who helped complete the bill on the final Winter Dance Party tour.

Had an ABC-Paramount release, *"Fake out"* that was described in '59 as a fast rising hit but certainly never got near the US Top 40 singles chart.

Not too certain what happened to him after the tour ended but as he was pursuing an acting career in tandem with his singing it is likely that part took over. Maybe somebody out there can supply more information on this fairly obscure artist?

SCHOOLS

Buddy's First school was the Roscoe Wilson Elementary School and he eventually transferred from there to the Roosevelt Elementary School.

In later years he first attended J. T. Hutchinson Junior High (with Bob Montgomery) and finally Lubbock High School from where he graduated - in the American sense - in 1955.

All the above schools were either in Lubbock itself or Lubbock County.

"THE SEARCHERS"

Film

Produced by John Ford, this famed western film featured 'Duke' John Wayne, who introduced the expression that caught the attention of impressionable young musicians in Lubbock, 1956 - *"That'll Be The Day"*.

Within a short space of time Buddy and Jerry Allison had written the words and music to what was - let's use the present tense, is - a classic bit of music.

"SEND ME SOME LOVIN"

Recorded by The Crickets (quartet) on 19th July 1957 at Norman Petty studios, Clovis, New Mexico

Written by John Marascolco and singer, Lloyd Price and was first recorded by Little Richard in 1956, being released as the flip of *"Lucille"* on Speciality 598. The 'B' side entered the Top 100 in the US during 1957 but it was not until 1963 that it became a Top 20 recording, courtesy of Sam Cooke.

The Crickets recording features the dubbed vocal backing of The Picks and became one of many great tracks used for 'The Chirping Crickets' album, 1958.

"SHAKE, RATTLE AND ROLL"

Practice tape; recorded in Lubbock, Texas late '56/early '57

Written by Jesse Stone aka Charles Calhoun, this song is rock'n'roll through and through. First charted as an R&B hit for Joe Turner in '54 in the US, it was then used by Bill Haley as his follow-up to *"Rock Around The Clock"*. (In the UK the Brunswick single of 'Shake' actually beat Haley's earlier single of 'Clock' into the charts).

The number is one of a handful of rock'n'roll numbers that would have been included in most self-respecting rockers stage-acts. Holly's version - from his earliest days - uses a compromise of the overtly sexual lyrics of Big Joe Turner's version and the sanitised Haley rendition.

The posthumous release of the Holly recording is heavily overdubbed instrumentally but has since seen release on Rollercoaster Records in its original basic mono format.

EARL SINKS

Texan performer who became a member of the post-Holly Crickets in 1958 and was lead singer on some of their very best material even if he is, naturally, somewhat overshadowed by the legacy of Buddy Holly.

In 1959 The Crickets version of *"Love's Made A Fool Of You"* was often mistakenly thought to feature Holly such was the similarity in styles. (Backing vocals were by The Roses, as in earlier days and the Crickets sound differed little from their first hits).

Earl Sinks also recorded as Earl Richards and Sinx Mitchell in a long, if rather low-key career, although he did have the occasional country hit in the US over the years.

"SLIPPIN AND SLIDIN"

Taped at Holly's New York flat, January 1959

Part composed by Richard Penniman himself the song was a minor 1956 hit for Little Richard in its own right, although it was only the flip of *"Long Tall Sally"* - a Top 10 record.

Holly experimented with slow and fast versions of *"Slippin' and Slidin'"* using both acoustic and electric guitar in his attempts. Later, it came to light that the slower version was meant to be played at double time so as to produce The Chipmunks sound! If this sounds far-fetched remember Alvin and gang was No. 1 in the US charts at that time.

A slow version, overdubbed by The Fireballs came out on the 'Reminiscing' album while the faster version came out years later on the 'Giant' LP. The undubbed versions as well as other takes have also been released (unofficially) over the years.

RONNIE SMITH

Headed a group in the '50s, Ronnie Smith and the Poor Boys, which included Carl Bunch who was to be seconded by Holly for the Winter Dance Party Tour after Jerry and Joe had decided to go their own way. In the Poor Boys at the same time was Tommy Allsup who also temporarily left to join Bunch and Jennings backing Buddy.

There was no acrimony in these arrangements and Ronnie Smith, from Odessa, Texas and Buddy were well known to each other. In an ironic twist Smith was re-united with his sidemen in early February when he was hired by the tour organisers to front Jennings/Allsup/Bunch and fulfil the remaining tour dates.

Ronnie Smith was always a minor artist although he recorded for several labels before he died a drugs-related death in the '60s.

"SMOKEY JOE'S CAFE"

Taped at Holly's New York flat, January 1959

A classic composition by the songwriting team of Jerry Leiber and Mike Stoller, *"Smokey Joe's Cafe"* was recorded by The Robins for Spark in 1955 eventually being released via Atco and creeping into the US Hot 100 at No. 79. But it has been termed a Coasters record ever since and is on most of their hit compilations.

Just before Holly left on his final, ill-fated tour in January of '59 he recorded several numbers that had been early favourites of his and *"Smokey Joe's Cafe"* was finally released, heavily overdubbed both instrumentally and vocally, on the 'Giant' album (1969).

Only in the last few years has the undubbed version been heard via bootleg-style releases.

"SOFT PLACE IN MY HEART"

Buddy and Bob performance at Nesman studio, Wichita Falls, Texas. Circa '54/'55

One of the earliest recordings which dates from the days when Buddy and his school pal Bob Montgomery, were playing fairly regularly at the Sunday Party on Radio KDAV, Lubbock, Texas. Composed by Montgomery the released track is over-dubbed somewhat in an attempt to give the track a commercial sound. In fact having both fiddle and steel guitar on the original performance indicates that Buddy and Bob were heavily country-oriented at the time. Certainly the audiences they were performing for on local Texas radio would have been expecting mainly country material.

Another version of *"Soft Place In My Heart"* exists dating from the same time-frame and is of poor quality.

TOMMY STEELE

Tommy Steele is an accomplished all-round entertainer who was born in Bermonsey, London the same year as Holly entered the world in Texas. Tommy was to spearhead the UK challenge to rock'n'roll supremacy and had major British chart success in 1956 whilst Holly was still searching for a breakthrough.

Steele - and Marty Wilde - ensured that the great Ritchie Valens would never enjoy major chart success over here by respectively taking the Valens compositions *"Come On Let's Go"* and *"Donna"* into the Top 10.

It seems Tommy Steele rated Buddy Holly highly and often featured a medley of his songs in stage or TV shows. These tributes eventually took some poetic licence with Tommy's accompanying monologue describing Buddy as a gangling giant of 6′ 4″! (He was actually a shade under six feet).

For many years Tommy talked of recording an album of Holly material but eventually his career veered away from recordings into musicals or production numbers. As a post-script Tommy Steele is still featuring Holly numbers on his nationwide 1994 tour and claims that he met Buddy in the U.S. during '56 when the latter was a little known artist on country tours.

"PAPPY" DAVE STONE

Dave Stone helped start the local Lubbock radio station, KDAV, on 19th September 1953 and remained part-owner for several years, thereafter. Like Hipockets Duncan and Ben Hall he had defected from radio KSEL to start the new venture. He also had a hand in getting Buddy his first big break which led to him obtaining a Nashville recording contract with Decca. Briefly, he was able to get the trio of Buddy, Bob and Larry on a Lubbock concert bill and this resulted in Eddie Crandall acting as the catalyst (see separate entry).

A very minor coincidence is that another Pappy - Pappy Daily a Houston distributor - was instrumental in getting the Big Bopper his original Mercury recording contract.

JESSE STONE

A legendary name from the early days who, apart from being a superlative arranger, also composed a number of classic rock'n'roll songs under the pseudonym, Charles Calhoun. Pick of the bunch is probably *"Shake, Rattle and Roll"*, followed closely by *"Money Honey"*.

He was arranger for Ray Charles in the '50s and - according to a letter Buddy wrote to Terry Noland on 14th December 1958 - Holly was already using Stone for arrangements . More likely is that Buddy was trying to line this up as we know that a gospel album was an unfulfilled project and Jesse Stone would have been the man for this.

It was almost certainly one of several projects that got permanently sidelined by the events of 3rd February 1959. Others included forming his own music company (Maria Music) and his record company (Prism Records). It is also suggested that he may have tried to set up a state of the art recording studio, perhaps with the help of his friend Snuff Garrett.

THE STRING-A-LONGS

Instrumental group produced by Norman Petty in Clovis who had a million-selling single in 1961 with the catchy *"Wheels"*. Composer credits were shown as Jimmy Torres and Richard Stephens both guitarists with the group which had first auditioned for Petty in 1960.

As we know Norman Petty's career didn't end in 1959 and his engineering skills were used to good effect in helping groups such as the Fireballs and String-a-Longs achieve hit status. He was involved in producing hundreds of recordings over the years usually leasing product to major labels but occasionally using his own small labels - see NORMAN AND VI PETTY entry.

ED SULLIVAN

Host of the major US TV series, the Ed Sullivan Show, he was a monolithic anchor man who introduced a coast to coast show that was equivalent in many ways to our own, Sunday Night at the London Palladium shows.

The Crickets made two guest appearances on the show, the first as a quartet in New York late '57 when they performed *"That'll Be The Day"* and *"Peggy Sue"*. Early in '58 - as a trio - they performed *"Oh Boy!"* and the surviving film clip is generally felt to be the best footage of Holly that exists.

It is interesting to compare both clips which were only filmed some eight weeks apart. Not only had Niki Sullivan departed the scene but Holly is by now sporting his trade-mark horn-rims and looks a more confident performer.

NIKI SULLIVAN

Born 1938 Southgate, California

Niki was a member of The Crickets almost continually during '57 and his main role was in playing rhythm guitar. In early photographs of the quartet Sullivan looks uncannily like Buddy - both wore spectacles but with Holly able to play either lead or rhythm guitar there was not much of a role for Sullivan who also had his own musical aspirations.

Sullivan was later to form his own group, The Plainsmen, but met with only limited success. After Buddy's death Niki teamed up with Gene Evans and recorded at Clovis under the name of The Hollyhawks. The group were managed by Lawrence Holley - Buddy's dad - for a short period in the '60s. (In another link it is known that Holly and Sullivan were distant cousins by marriage).

Sullivan remains a warm, emotional man who has the fondest memories of his days with the group that nothing can tarnish. His input into the Crickets, has been musically modest, but he was an essential ingredient in the group's sound and visual presentation. He received belated recognition in 1986 when, along with Jerry, Joe and Sonny, he was inducted to Lubbock's Walk of Fame - like those three, his part in the group was omitted from the film biog. Although he was probably relieved not to be called Jess or Ray Bob.

It was a revelation in 1983 to hear the original, undubbed version of *"Maybe Baby"* on which Niki's second vocal line comes across loud and clear. Although he left the group prematurely he has the consolation of appearing on a handful of Holly's greatest ever recordings.

SUN RECORDS

Whole books have been written on the subject of Sun Records, the Memphis label started by Sam Phillips back in 1952 - see entry under SAM PHILLIPS.

It is fairly certain that Buddy never knocked on that particular door, although from the South and residing close - in US terms - to Tennessee. But he often drove through Memphis during 1956 en route to his Nashville sessions from his Lubbock home. Who knows, perhaps he did try and make contact. Meanwhile his friend and idol Elvis, had temporarily transferred his own recording operations up to New York for the famous *"Hound Dog"* session.

Sun Records holds a quite unique place in the history of rock'n'roll and will not be forgotten while the music itself lives.

"TAKE THESE SHACKLES FROM MY HEART"

Home recording by Buddy Holley and Bob Montgomery, circa 1952

One of the very earliest Holly vocal attempts in duet with his school pal, Bob Montgomery.

The recording takes the form of a very rough acetate indeed and its release would be academic only. Incidentally the song is an early country number and is not to be confused with the later Hank William's number, *"Take These Chains From My Heart"*.

"TAKE YOUR TIME"

Recorded following Niki Sullivan's departure at Norman Petty Studios, Clovis, New Mexico. Probably 14th February 1958

Released as the flip of *"Rave On"* this song was not recorded at the New York session but several weeks later in Clovis after the group had returned from their highly successful Australian tour.

The number was written by Holly in collaboration with Norman who plays a prominent organ throughout. A Holly discography reveals that Jerry was keeping the moderato tempo going via a cardboard box and the overall sound is a good one.

As most fans know the Crickets and Holly recordings are virtually indistinguishable and at this particular recording session the other two numbers (*"Fools Paradise/"Think It Over"*) were released under the Crickets banner - the subtle difference being the dubbing of background vocals from The Roses.

Rehearsal tapes of *"Take Your Time"* and others have been put out as unsanctioned releases and make for interesting listening as they are interspersed with occasional studio chat that allows the listener to be a fly-on-the-wall eavesdropper.

"TELL ME HOW"

Recorded at Norman Petty Studios, Clovis, New Mexico between May and July '57. The Crickets release as a quartet.

This has to be one of the greatest 'B' sides ever released (flip of *"Maybe Baby"*) and is an example of the Crickets at the very height of their creativity. Holly's unique lead guitar solo appears to be played on the bass string of his Fender and its one of those small changes that - to a layman - smacks of pure genius.

Writing is credited to Holly, Jerry Allison and Norman Petty and instead of the sheet music ending up under the MPL banner it remains with Sherwin Music. Not quite certain why as of this writing.

A recording that has seldom been covered by other artists and it remains one of those gems that surely deserved greater air play over the years. We all know that if a Holly/Crickets number is played on the radio it is invariably one of a select band of numbers. Tell me how many times you've heard this song featured?

"THAT'LL BE THE DAY"

Hit version recorded as a demo on 24th/25th February 1957 at the Norman Petty Studios, Clovis, New Mexico. See below re: personnel

Generally acknowledged to have been written by Buddy and drummer Jerry Allison shortly after attending a John Wayne movie (see entry THE SEARCHERS), it was first recorded in Nashville and came out in the US as the flip of *"Ollie Vee"* just two weeks after the Crickets hit version entered their charts. Those must have been confusing days for any US record fans who happened to purchase both singles - one a ponderous version by the little known Buddy Holly and the other a much slicker version on Brunswick by the totally unknown Crickets.

Amazingly the chart-topping version is no more than a demo, recorded in Clovis shortly before Joe B Mauldin became a full-time group member and with backing vocals by friends June Clark, Gary and Ramona Tollett and Niki Sullivan. The record was a million seller reaching No. 1 on both sides of the Atlantic and was belatedly certified gold in 1969.

In America Decca put out all the Nashville material in 1958 on an album entitled *"That'll Be The Day"* in an effort to cash in on The Crickets big hit. Frustratingly fans in the UK had to wait till late 1961 before the album was released, although some of the recordings had come out on hard to find EP's.

Two live version of *"That'll Be The Day"* are available - the first from the Crickets 1957 appearance on the Ed Sullivan Show and a poorly recorded version from their UK appearance at The London Palladium in March '58 when they raced through three numbers on their UK TV debut.

Also available on a bootleg-style album, are short jingles sung by The Crickets with the words of the hit song adapted as a 'thank you' to Bob Theile and Murray Deutch, who had done so much to help launch and promote the disc.

"That'll Be The Day" doubtless inspired the 1973 film/book by Ray Connolly that became a very popular release despite not being able to use the hit record in the sound-track - Bobby Vee's version was included instead.

Back in 1957 The Tunettes did the usual Embassy (Woolworths) version whilst a UK cover by Larry Page got nowhere. Years later the Everlys had a '60s UK chart version and Linda Ronstadt had a major hit in the US the following decade. The song had been covered by a diverse variety of recording artists over the years.

Strangely an unsuccessful US lawsuit was brought in the '80s claiming that Holly's version plagiarised a song others had written. The plaintiffs apparently waited 30 years too long before bringing the case.

"THAT MAKES IT TOUGH"

Recorded at Holly's New York flat, 8th December 1958

Another of the half dozen compositions that Holly sang into his Ampex tape recorder just before Christmas 1958. The Ampex had been bought from Norman Petty who had used it commercially so it was by no means the run of the mill domestic machine.

"That Makes It Tough" ended up as a posthumous release being the 'B' side of *"Learning The Game"* which became a short-lived hit single in late 1960. All the six tracks that Holly was working on were then incorporated in the second volume of the 'Story' album which hit the shops here in November 1960. (With Buddy far more popular here than in the States the LP had, infuriatingly, been released many months earlier over there).

The original single version was the Jack Hansen overdub and the later overdub engineered by Norman Petty did not have an LP release here until the 'Remember' album came out. All three versions, including the undubbed one, came out as part of the MCA box set several years back.

"THAT'S MY DESIRE"

Recorded at Bell Sound Studios, New York on 25th January 1958. Jerry and Joe B backing musicians with Al Caiola (guitar) and Norman Petty, piano. Background vocals - session singers.

Written by Carroll Loveday and Helmy Kresa in 1931, this ballad has become an evergreen and Holly was by no means the only rock artist to try it. Eddie Cochran had recorded it in 1956 while Elvis had sung it during his Million Dollar Quartet session. Earlier, both Frankie Laine and Sammy Kaye had versions which entered the Top 10 US Billboard charts -the strong lyrics not falling foul of the censor unlike some much more innocuous material in the '50s.

Holly's version was recorded at the same session as *"Rave On"* but was to remain unreleased for 8 years until it emerged (overdubbed by Norman Petty) as the flip of the alternate *"Maybe Baby"*. Buddy Holly's version didn't appear to do him, or the song, justice and it was largely ignored, although interestingly it was a minor revelation years later to finally hear the undubbed version which - strangely - lacked the slightly discordant sound of the dubbed release and was a vast improvement.

Recently out-takes of Buddy singing the number, prior to completing the finished take, have been released on a European album.

"THAT'S WHAT THEY SAY"

Taped at Holly's New York flat, 3rd December 1958, Take 2.

One of Holly's new compositions that he had recorded with simple acoustic guitar accompaniment in his New York flat, late '58. Appeared, overdubbed by Jack Hansen, as part of the 'Story Volume 2 LP before being used as the flip of *"What To Do"* in 1961, which became a minor hit. The Petty dubbed version came out years later on the 'Remember' album while the undubbed version has never had an official release.

It did, however appear on a bootleg-style 'Apartment Tapes' album recently, but with no trace of Take 1 which supposedly exists.

BOB THEILE

It's almost a case of saying see the entry under Murray Deutch as their names are always linked together when Holly's name comes up. In fact, Bob was the A&R man for the record company (Coral) whereas his compatriot was on the music publishing side of things over at Peers - Southern. Both had a hand in getting Holly's career launched and have talked disarmingly on the subject in subsequent interviews.

Theile had a jazz pedigree and his job could not have been harder for him and others, when rock'n'roll began to saturate the airwaves. Coral's roster of stars included million-selling artists such as Teresa Brewer, The McGuire Sisters and Don Cornell but nevertheless the times were a - changing and they (Decca/Coral) quickly obtained their market share of the new sound via Holly/Haley/The Kalin Twins and others.

Whether Holly would have remained with Coral (now MCA) is interesting to speculate. Certainly MCA have their critics when it comes to releasing Holly products which has been very uneven indeed over the years.

"THINK IT OVER"

Crickets recording, following Niki Sullivan's departure at Norman Petty's Studios, Clovis, New Mexico. Probably 14th February 1958. Vi Petty on piano

Written by Buddy, Jerry and Norman Petty this was the last Crickets recording to go Top 40 in the States, reaching a lowly No. 27. In the UK the record was much more popular reaching No. 11 and spending virtually two months in the charts.

Interestingly, Holly, ever innovative, moved away from the standard guitar break and instead Vi Petty treated the record buyer to a fascinating piano-roll solo. Even now I can remember Luxembourg DJ Pete Murray spinning the record again and again just to listen to the unique piano sound.

The finished hit recording was transformed into a Crickets release courtesy of The Roses added backing vocals. In the last few years studio out-takes of this number in rehearsal have been (unofficially) released and studio dialogue helps to show how the boys would often creatively work up an arrangement as they went along.

Seldom covered, it is worth looking out for the Bobby Fuller Four version where the vocals are similar but a stinging guitar solo galvanises the recording mid-way through and the change works well.

THREE STARS

If *"Tribute To Buddy Holly"* is the definitive paean to Holly then surely *"Three Stars"* is the most memorable where the triumvirate of artists is concerned (but see TRIBUTE RECORDS entry).

The US hit version was by Radio KFXM, San Bernadino, DJ Tommy Dee who was moved by the tragedy to pen the number the day after the accident. His recording had vocal accompaniment by Carol Kay and the Teen-aires who were session musicians with the label (Crest). In the UK Ruby Wright - last in the charts with *"Bimbo"*, 1954 (!) - had the hit on the Parlophone label.

Surely the most heartrending version is that by Eddie Cochran which was cut at Gold Star on 5th February with the finished master said to be made up from eight separate takes. Perhaps too traumatic to release when recorded it came out as a posthumous single in 1966.

THE THREE TUNES

One of the early band name for the musicians who backed Buddy. Apparently the name was not used on the bandstand but it did end up on a record label (US Decca single, *"Ting-a-Ling"*).

Before the Crickets became an established quartet in '57, various local Lubbock musicians had played back-up and the whole situation tended to be a bit fluid. Amongst the names used in addition to the above were The Two Tones, Buddy and Bob and The Rhythm Playboys.

"TING-A-LING"

Recorded at second Nashville recording session, Bradley's Barn, 22nd July 1956

One of the best of Holly's largely abortive Nashville sessions was his different interpretation of the old Clovers 1952 hit *"Ting-a-Ling"*. Holly's release was eventually credited to Nugetre - Ahmet Ertegun, Atlantic mogul's pseudonym - and it was belatedly issued as a single in the US as an obvious attempt by Decca to jump on the Holly/Crickets bandwagon. At its peak in mid-1958. Strangely the single was released with the description, *"Buddy Holly and The Three Tunes"* (see previous entry).

It's first UK release was a posthumous one on a Brunswick EP before ending up on the budget-priced Ace Of Hearts album 'That'll Be The Day'.

With Earl Sinks on vocals the post-Holly Crickets also did a particularly powerful version of the number in 1959. In the muddled world of composer credits the song was listed as composed by Cedarwood's Jim Denny before - eventually - getting its rightful Nugetre accreditation. (In mitigation the Holly recording bears only passing resemblance to The Clovers versions).

GARY AND RAMONA TOLLETT

These names have a brief but significant place in the Buddy Holly story. In February 1957 Gary Tollett recorded a couple of Clovis demos under the name of Gary Dale and playing lead guitar/drums on the date were Buddy Holly and Jerry Allison respectively. Gary's wife, Ramona, along with June Clark and Niki Sullivan helped out on backing vocals and it seemed fairly logical for the Tolletts' to reciprocate a few days later when Buddy and Jerry were cutting their own demo, *"That'll Be The Day"*.

In March '57 the Tolletts' had a further session, the tracks of which remained unissued until they recently appeared on a European bootleg-style album. The tracks are quite collectable, featuring as they do Buddy and Jerry as backing musicians.

Sadly the Tolletts' themselves lost a son a few years ago, the victim of a light plane crash.

GEORGE TOMSCO

Lead guitarist with the Fireballs instrumental group that had a number of US hits in the '60s all of which were recorded under the direction of Norman Petty at Clovis. Jimmy Gilmer joined the group as vocalist in 1961 and they had a massive hit with *"Sugar Shack"* (see entry under JIMMY GILMER).

In the '60s Tomsco helped on The Buddy Holly Songbook project with Tommy Allsup and also assisted the Fireballs with a whole series of posthumous overdubs of Holly material. This ranged from the earliest Buddy and Bob material through to the tapes Holly had left in New York on his portable tape machine, just days before he joined up with the 1959 Winter Dance Party tour.

Tomsco is a talented musician and he also found time to compose much of the instrumental material that both The Fireballs and The String-a-longs issued - see separate entries.

TOURS

Buddy Holly - as a member of a group, never on a solo basis - toured almost continuously from the time he hit the charts in August '57 with *"That'll Be The Day"*. He had also undertaken three tours during '56 , playing dates in Southern states and with the roster of artists exclusively country-based. (Needless to say without a hit to their name Buddy and the boys were very much a support act.)

There were two major overseas tours during '58 (UK and Australia) and as we know, a 1959 tour of Britain was felt to be a certainty with exploratory talks having taken place between Leslie Grade, in this country and US tour promoter Irving Feld.

One ironic footnote - when researching this book it was discovered that the Winter Dance Party was Holly's 13th tour.

TRIBUTE RECORDS

Years ago a US publication listed more than twenty different Tribute records which directly referred to the February '59 Iowa's plane crash. The majority of these were eulogies to Buddy Holly but some referred to all three stars (*"The Great Tragedy"* / *"Three Young Men"*, *"Three Stars"* etc.)

Even thicker on the ground have been tracks which mention Holly fleetingly in the lyrics. Probably the most famous of all 'tribute' records is *"American Pie"* which, cleverly manages not to mention Holly's name at all, although Don McLean has always said that Buddy was the inspiration behind the recording (His 'American Pie' album is dedicated to the singer).

Over the years records which have alluded to Holly in their lyrics have outnumbered those mentioning Valens and Bopper by about 10 to 1. But at the time of the fatal crash, Valens was often mentioned in the US media as being the major star by virtue of his having had a hit currently in the charts.

LARRY TRIDER

One of the least known, one-time member of the post-Holly Crickets who originated from Lazbuddie, West Texas, but didn't actually get to record with the group. Consequently he rarely received a mention on sleeve-notes appertaining to the Crickets, although this has been remedied in more recent years.

When the group were getting towards the end of their Liberty days (1965) and with Jerry Naylor sidelined, Larry and Jerry Allison got together to tour as The Crickets but as a duo sometimes supplemented by one or two friends. After some 18 months together they amicably split although both remained in the music business.

Even earlier Trider had worked around both Clovis and Lubbock and was a true contemporary of Holly's. He cut his first record in Petty's studio back in 1961 but that failed to open doors.

Had a lengthy musical stint at the Golden Nugget casino in Las Vegas during the '70s before eventually gravitating back to the West Texas music scene where he still performs.

Buddy Holly, backstage with two young fans, Green Bay, Wisconsin, 1st Feb. '58.

"TRUE LOVE WAYS"

With the Dick Jacob's Orchestra; recorded in stereo at Coral Record Studios, Pythian Temple, New York, 21st October 1958

Written by Buddy with the help of Norman Petty the song was composed specifically for Buddy's wife Maria. The melody was supposedly based on a gospel tune *"I'll Be All Right"*, a particular favourite of Holly's as recorded by The Angelic Gospel Singers - see separate entry.

This last session of Buddy's produced his only recordings with strings and he has often - mistakenly - been given credit as the first rock artist to use a full orchestral backing. Whilst he was ever innovative acts such as The Platters had used orchestral backings from around 1956.

What is surprising is that *"True Love Ways"* did not make the Top 20 when released in 1960 although it has subsequently been recognised as probably Holly's greatest vocal performance. The song has become an evergreen through the years and it briefly became a US country No. 1 in 1980 courtesy of Mickey Gilley. (The recordings by Holly/Gilley were in the same key and tempo and the tapes could have been used to construct a duet!)

Both stereo and mono masters were made from Holly's recording. The stereo cut was used in a Terry's All gold TV advert in 1988 and consequently the single was re-released and spent four weeks in the Top 75 list.

The Picks have released the Holly recording with their dubbed vocal sounds but the backing is intrusive and is recommended but only with reservations.

JOE TURNER

Born 18th May 1911 in Missouri Big Joe Turner became one of the greatest pre-war blues-shouters and appeared with such famous band-leaders as Bennie Moten and Count Basie.

At the breakout of rock'n'roll - although well in his '40s - he hitched his star to the trend having already had a string of early '50s hits in the R&B charts. *"Shake Rattle and Roll"* on Atlantic 1026 then crossed over and became his biggest pop hit during 1954. Buddy's 1956 demo of the number appears to be a hybrid of Turner's raunchy version and the more antiseptic lyrics of Bill Haley.

Not known whether Holly and Turner ever met although biographical notes on Turner indicate he undertook several Alan Freed tours in the mid-'50s.

Joe Turner died 23rd November 1985 having continued to perform for several years despite deteriorating health.

UK TOUR - MARCH 1958

The Crickets flew in to England late February for what was to be a most successful four week tour. Always referred to as a UK, or British tour, it criss crossed England, the only venue outside the country being on 24th March in Cardiff, Wales. For many years there were rumours that the group had stopped off in Ireland but this was not the case.

There is a well-researched booklet entitled 'Buddy In Britain' that was published by John Firminger of The Crickets File which is recommended reading.

The UK tour roster comprised Gary Miller, the Tanner Sisters, Des O'Connor and Ronnie Keene and his Orchestra. The Lew and Leslie Grade bill was headed by Buddy Holly and the Crickets - the only US act on what was basically a traditional variety or music-hall show.

RITCHIE VALENS

Born Richard Steven Valenzuela on 13th May 1941 probably the most startling fact in this book is Valens age - just 17

At the time of the fatal plane crash Valens was by far the hottest of the three artists in terms of chart action. His double-sided hit *"Donna"/"La Bamba"* had entered the lists in the December and was at No. 3 on February 3rd. It subsequently peaked at No. 2 on the Billboard charts. In contrast, Holly's career in the States was fairly moribund with his last real hit having been some six months previous.

Valens had a plaintive voice and played superb guitar, although on most recording sessions Rene Hall played lead and Ritchie played rhythm. Just days after the accident Del-fi released two of Valens solo instrumentals on a single and for some reason used the pseudonym - Arvee Allens. (Get it?) The record failed to chart which was no surprise.

Ritchie has had a small renaissance in popularity following the release of the 1987 film biography, 'La Bamba'. This led to re-issues of the very small catalogue of material Valens had recorded and also brought him his first UK hit for 28 years (*'La Bamba'* peaked at No. 49). Much more exciting, for real oldies fans, was the recent discovery of numerous studio rehearsals by Valens which were released on a CD entitled 'The Lost Tapes'. As if the discovery of thirty-odd 'recordings' were not enough, many were in rudimentary stereo.

Valens is remembered moderately well in this country when he is not being confused with the English singer, Ricky Valance, who had a brief chart success of his own in 1960. However it is frustrating that portrayals of Valens invariably picture him as a hip-swivelling Latin-type Elvis, where all photographic and celluloid material from the '50s projects a totally different image.

"VALLEY OF TEARS"

Recorded at Norman Petty Studios, Clovis, New Mexico between May and July 1957. Trio supplemented by Norman Petty, organ and Vi Petty, piano

"Valley Of Tears" was composed by Fats Domino and producer, Dave Bartholomew and became a major hit for Fats in May 1957. Evidently brother Larry Holley suggested that Buddy try the number and it went into the can to be released in '58 as part of Holly's only solo album put out during his lifetime.

In 1961 it was released posthumously as the flip of *"You're so Square"* and the single was surprisingly a double-sided UK hit. (Surprising given that most fans would have already had both the Holly recordings in their collections).

See also comments under FATS DOMINO.

JACK VAUGHN

Jack Vaughn was the third member of the Norman Petty Trio along with Norman and wife, Vi. Jack was a local musician who played guitar in the group, which had a $^1/_2$ million-seller in 1954 with *"Mood Indigo"* and a string of other releases on the Columbia label.

Sadly, Jack died in 1984 - the same year as Norman passed on.

BOBBY VEE

If any one person in the world believes in fate that individual is surely Bobby Vee. Not only did he and his group The Shadows make their professional debut on the Winter Dance Party - as a direct result of the fatal crash - but Bobby Vee performed in a style that almost out-hiccuped Buddy Holly.

His performance on 3rd February 1959 at the Moorhead, Minnesota concert was to be a stepping-stone to fame and fortune. In fact he became quite a teenage rage for several years in the States, clocking up far more hits than Holly ever did - although he had a decade to try.

Bobby Vee is a genuine and sincere fan of Holly and has always been ready to give the Texan full credit. Bobby still performs but he has veered towards a cabaret-style act these days. On record the 'Bobby Vee Meets The Crickets' album was a major hit in '62 but his later LP 'Tribute To Buddy Holly' did not chart. Always in demand for anniversary-type concerts Bobby also continues to link up with the Crickets on occasion and of late has recorded a superb Holly medley with them - check out Rollercoaster 45 RRC 2009,

Bobby Vee was born Robert Velline on 3rd April 1943 in Fargo, North Dakota - Holly was actually flying to the town of Fargo at the time of the fatal crash.

GENE VINCENT

Vincent Eugene Craddock was born 11th February 1935 in Norfolk, Virginia and was surely one of the greatest of all rock'n'roll performers. His name is inextricably linked with that of Eddie Cochran for reasons any self-respecting fan is aware (e.g. toured together/almost died together).

Vincent and the Blue Caps had met Holly briefly when on tour in New Mexico and both artists are cited as having Eddie Cochran among their best friends. Vincent and Holly also both cut their first professional sessions at the same studios in Nashville in early '56. Any other links between Holly and Vincent are tenuous but the latter recorded the Johnny Burnette composition *"My Heart"* which is very Holly-esque, while in later years Gene listed Buddy Holly's name in cataloguing the stars in Jim Pewter's *"Story Of The Rockers"*. Certainly Holly and The Crickets sang *"Be-Bop-A-Lula"* as part of their stage act during '57/'58, but probably many contemporaries did too.

Gene never lost faith in rock'n'roll and it was tragedy that he died too soon, on 12th October 1971 of bleeding ulcers and is buried in the Eternal Valley Memorial Park near Los Angeles in California.

VIOLIN

Early publicity information stressed that this was Buddy's earliest musical instrument before switching to guitar. In fact he more often practised on piano and drums from an early age eventually shifting to mandolin and guitar.

Apparently Holly sat in on drums with Dion and the Belmonts once or twice during the final tour after Carl Bunch caught frostbite and was sidelined. But his great love and talent was for the guitar. The makes he played are listed under a separate entry - see GUITARS.

"WAIT TILL THE SUN SHINES NELLIE"

Taped at Holly's New York flat between 1st and 22nd January 1959

Buddy strummed a short version of this oldie into his tape recorder just before setting out on his 13th and last tour in January '59. Evidently the number was a pre-war favourite of his mother having been composed by the songwriting partnership of Andrew Sterling and Harry Von Tilzer. Whether Buddy would have recorded the number commercially we do not know. It seems unlikely.

Heavily overdubbed by The Fireballs and with ponderous backing vocals the number was released in '62 as the flipside of *"Reminiscing"* which scored heavily in the singles charts. This Coral single on Q 72455 is worth seeking out as it has less instrumental overdubbing than the album release. (Extra guitar had been added for the stereo LP release).

Undubbed and back to its stark 70 seconds, the number has appeared recently on the unsanctioned 'Apartment Tapes' album.

LARRY WELBORN

Bass player on the hit version of *"That'll Be The Day"*, Larry was a member of the Buddy and Bob line-up and is on a whole stack of early tracks that pre-date both the Coral and Decca recordings.

Whilst not well-known as a solo performer he is proficient on many instruments and was also drafted into the Crickets for a period in the '60s. Still alive and well and has belatedly been involved in Holly anniversary celebrations.

"WELL . . . ALL RIGHT"

Recorded at Norman Petty Studios, Clovis, approx. 14th February 1958. Trio included Jerry Allison on cymbals.

All three Crickets are listed as composers with Norman Petty, of this quite classic number. Only issued as a 'B' side to *"Heartbeat"* it is one of several numbers that would probably have charted if released in its own right.

Composed as a direct result of listening to Little Richard continually shout the phrase backstage at the Paramount theatre, New York, the lyrics are surprisingly introspective even if tear-jerkingly simple. That the number was not included on the Holly 'Love Songs' compilation defies belief.

Recorded by many artists over the years Blind Faith did their interpretation while Santana had a very small UK hit with it in 1978. The Crickets have used it in their stage act over the years but have favoured a flat-out rhythmic interpretation.

Of the 21 recordings overdubbed by The Picks of Holly material released a few years back this one works quite well.

SONNY WEST

Singer songwriter, who with Bill Tilghman, composed two of Holly's most memorable recordings, *"Oh Boy!"* and *"Rave On"*.

Sonny had several single releases himself over the years including his version of *"Rave On"* on Atlantic records. It is a likeable version but lacks the power and intensity of Holly's performance.

As a performer West is best remembered for his classic rockabilly recording of *"Rock-ola Baby"* which Norman Petty produced in his Clovis studio.

"WHAT TO DO"

Taped at Buddy Holly's New York flat on 3rd December 1958

One of the half-dozen self-compositions that Buddy recorded at home on his Ampex tape machine. It was given to Dick Jacobs and subsequently overdubbed by Jack Hansen with orchestra and chorus and became a minor hit when released as a single in 1961 (Coral Q 72419).

Two years later a much superior version (Coral Q 72469) with instrumental over-dubbing by Norman Petty and with Holly's vocal given more echo, was released and charted again. Meanwhile the undubbed version has only been heard on the unsanctioned 'Apartment Tapes' album, to date.

HANK WILLIAMS

Born 17th September 1923

Probably the most legendary male country singer of all time. His immortality is assured following his early death at 29 on the first day of January 1953. Holly would have been an impressionable 16 at that time and was already performing locally around the Lubbock area.

Buddy was certainly influenced by Hank during those formative years, although, unfortunately he never recorded any of Hank's material, unlike several of his Southern counterparts (Cash/Lewis/Orbison etc.).

One thing Holly and Williams do share is the heavy irony of their last studio recordings. For Hank it was the prophetic *"I'll Never Get Out Of This World Alive"* while Buddy was more pointed claiming *"It Doesn't Matter Anymore"*.

It was strange to learn that Hank's widow, Billie Jean, was to subsequently marry Johnny Horton, only to be widowed a second time. Incidentally, both Hank Williams and Buddy have had Hollywood biopics immortalising their career. If Busey was an unlikely screen Holly then reflect that Hank was played by actor George Hamilton.

See also entry-JOHNNY HORTON.

LARRY WILLIAMS

Born Lawrence E Williams on 10th May 1935 Larry Williams was one of the archetypal stars of primitive rock'n'roll although his hit recordings were thin on the ground. He had two Speciality singles in the charts during 1957 and it all was downhill thereafter.

In 1958 he was on the Alan Freed Big Beat show along with The Crickets, Jerry Lee, Chuck Berry and others. In later years he drifted back to the R&B circuit which he had deserted in 1955 when joining Lloyd Price's band.

Almost all Larry William's Speciality recordings are self-compositions including one entitled *"Ting-a-Ling"*. A quite different song to that of Holly or The Robins.

Sadly Williams committed suicide in 1980 at the age of 44. It has been said that his lifestyle was both flamboyant and somewhat chequered.

CHUCK WILLIS

One of the few rock'n'roll artists to pre-decease Buddy Holly - Johnny Ace was probably the first. For many years the cause of his death was obscure but the definitive Chuck Willis box set is clear; it was peritonitis following abdominal surgery on 10th April 1958.

The Crickets recorded a masterly version of the Willis composition *"It's Too Late"* but other connections between the artists are few. Chuck did use Jesse Stone (see separate entry) around '56/'57 as arranger on the sessions that produced *"Juanita"* and *"C C Rider"*.

Always mentioned is their ironic choice of final record releases during their respective lifetimes. If *"It Doesn't Matter Anymore"* was vaguely prophetic then Chuck Willis went overboard with his two-sided biggie *"What Am I Living For"* and *"Hang-up My Rock'n'Roll Shoes"*.

Also worth mentioning is the involvement of King Curtis on tenor sax at Chuck's last session (14th February 1958). Willis had been born 30 years earlier on 31st January 1928 in Atlanta, Georgia.

BOB WILLS

Texan band leader who was rightly dubbed the King of Western Swing and his style has been heavily influential throughout the years. Born in 1905 he was to eventually name his band the Texas Playboys and among his acolytes can be named such country luminaries as Merle Haggard, Waylon Jennings and Tommy Allsup (courtesy of Asleep at the Wheel).

There is little doubt that Holly was influenced by Bob Wills in the early years and like Wills, used a fiddle in his early line-ups. (Not forgetting Holly's briefly used name The Rhythm Playboys).

Waylon Jennings said all when he composed and recorded *"Bob Wills Is Still The King"*. Wills died 13th May 1975 in Fort Worth, Texas.

JOHN 'PEANUTS' WILSON

Deserves a mention as joint composer with Roy Orbison of the Crickets *"You've Got Love"*, the track often mentioned as containing the best of all Holly guitar solos.

Johnny Wilson was a member of Orbison's group The Teen Kings in the early years before adopting the nickname Peanuts and releasing the Brunswick single *"Cast Iron Arm"/"You've Got Love"*. Never a national hit, it has nevertheless been recognised as a true classic of its era.

In later years became a songwriter of note composing *"Love The World Away"* by Kenny Rogers which was used in the 'Urban Cowboy' movie.

Johnny Wilson died in the early '80s.

"WISHING"

Recorded at Norman Petty's Clovis, New Mexico studios, July/August 1958. Tommy Allsup, lead guitar, Jerry and Joe replaced by session-men

Written by Buddy and friend, Bob Montgomery *"Wishing"* was one of two compositions which they hoped would be recorded by the Everly brothers, who had just hit No. 1 with *"Bird Dog"*. Unfortunately this did not happen but fine demos were recorded by Buddy in Clovis and both eventually came out on singles.

Released in the UK in 1963, *"Wishing"* was one of a hat-trick of posthumous Top 10 hits that Holly had that year. An absolutely amazing performance that gave the answer to earlier critics who had said that interest in Holly's music would be short-lived morbid curiosity.

The UK single is worth searching out as it comes without the additional guitar overdubbing which was used on the album release ('Holly In The Hills') and most subsequent re-issues.

It is certain that Holly recorded the definitive version of *"Wishing"* and it has seldom been covered.

"WORDS OF LOVE"

Recorded at Norman Petty Studios, Clovis, New Mexico on 8th April 1957. Personnel: Buddy, Jerry and Joe B Mauldin

One of Buddy Holly's greatest-ever compositions it became his first US Coral release in 1957 and - incredibly - made little impact at the time. Instead the Diamonds cover version was briefly a hit, peaking at No. 13 in July 1957.

"Words Of Love" didn't even rate a release over here and UK fans were left to discover it on side two of Holly's first solo album the following year. Four of these fans were embryonic singers known as The Quarrymen and eventually their 1964 recording was issued on their 'Beatles For Sale' album. Forever after it has been accepted as a song years ahead of its time and has been a perennial favourite. (Not being released here didn't stop it being included on the hit '20 Golden Greats' LP).

On his recording Buddy used his own overdubbed harmony vocal which was very innovative in those monaural days. Holly also used both acoustic and electric guitar on the track. The month before the April studio session Holly had practised the number and a very sub-standard recording of part of his performance has been in circulation for several years.

According to Jerry Allison the vocal and guitar sound that they achieved on *"Words Of Love"* was influenced greatly by the US duo, Mickey and Sylvia. The song itself bears more than a passing resemblance to their hit *"Love Is Strange"*.

"YOU AND I ARE THROUGH"

'Buddy and Bob' performance at radio station KDAV. Circa '54/'55

Written by Bob Montgomery this was one of several country-style numbers that was released in 1965 on the 'Holly In The Hills' album. It seemed to fans - at the time - that the wealth of posthumous releases was exhausted although years later devotees were delighted by the release of several other recordings via the 'Giant' album.

The Master recording of *"You And I Are Through"* has unidentified overdubbing on it, in an attempt to give the record a better sound. A further poorly recorded version of the number by Buddy and Bob has circulated among fans for several years but has not been commercially released.

"YOU ARE MY ONE DESIRE"

Recorded at the third and final Nashville recording session at Bradley's Barn on 15th November 1956

Written by bassist Don Guess, who played on the session, this was one of only two ballads that Holly attempted for Decca. None of the Decca material was successful apart from the posthumous UK release of *"Midnight Shift"* on their Brunswick subsidiary.

The false start at the beginning of the issued Take 2 has been included on the European bootleg-style album 'The Greatest And the Latest'. It is probably of academic interest to even the most devout fans.

"You Are My One Desire" is rather a stark recording with a prominent 'cling-cling' piano backing. The Picks dubbed vocal backings were added behind Holly's voice for a 1986 album release and gave the track a much better and fuller sound.

"YOU'RE THE ONE"

Written and recorded Christmas 1958 at radio KLLL, Lubbock, Texas. Personnel: Holly (vocals), Waylon Jennings and Slim Corbin - handclaps

Evidently written quite spontaneously when Holly met up with his friends Waylon Jennings and Slim Corbin who were connected with the local radio station, call sign K-Triple-L. The short number featured Holly accompanying himself on guitar whilst the others clapped a snappy rhythm. Fortunately the tape was kept in its original form and released in 1964 as part of the "*Showcase*" album. Much later a heavily overdubbed version was put out as part of the "*Giant*" album.

"YOU'VE GOT LOVE"

Recorded on the road, Oklahoma City, USA late Sept '57. Crickets were a quartet at the time

One of the many marvellous tracks that came out on '*The Chirping Crickets*' album in 1958 in the days when the Crickets really did 'chirp' courtesy of The Picks or The Roses. The track was one of a quartet that The Crickets recorded when they met up on tour with Norman Petty who 'borrowed' a US airforce base to set-up his mobile recording equipment. Later the dubbed backing vocals of The Picks gave the track its finished sound.

Holly plays a ringing guitar solo on the number that had been written by fellow-Texans Roy Orbison and Teen King member Johnny Wilson. Months earlier Johnny 'Peanuts' Wilson had recorded his own version as the flip of "*Cast Iron Arm*".

The Holly/Crickets version got belated recognition as a minor hit single when released in 1964.

ZAGER AND EVANS

Denny Zager and Rick Evans, recorded "*In The Year 2525*" several years back and it was a giant hit.

It's been said that Holly's music is timeless and it certainly looks poised to live and flourish as we stand on the brink of the 21st Century. We can only hope that its still being heard when the 26th one eventually rolls into view. Who knows?

That'll be the day.

Afterword

It is possible that this volume will one day be revised and updated and if so perhaps a fully illustrated version will be considered.

Meanwhile anyone wishing to contact the author with suggestions, corrections and brickbats are invited to write to the under-mentioned address : -

Alan J Mann

PO Box 17

Little Melton

Norwich, NR9 3PA

Strenuous efforts have been taken to avoid the infringement of any copyright in the preparation of this book. In the case of any oversight my humble apologies are offered.

The Author

Born in Norwich in 1939, Alan Mann spent his working life in the banking industry before accepting early retirement in 1993. A fan of American rock'n'roll music since the '50s , he has always had a particular interest in Buddy Holly's music and finally visited Lubbock, Texas in late 1986.

Over the years he has written the occasional article in fan magazines but this is his first and doubtless last, full-length work.

This 'A-Z of Buddy Holly' copyright Alan Mann, 1994.
Printed by Norwich Colourprint Limited